Beautiful
GALWAY
Connemara & The Burren

Featuring the photography of Michael Diggin,
Irish Tourist Board/Bord Fáilte and Colour Library Books

Published in Ireland by
Gill & Macmillan Ltd, Goldenbridge, Dublin 8
with associated companies around the world

© 1993 Colour Library Books Ltd, Godalming, Surrey
Printed and bound in Singapore by Tien Wah Press
ISBN 0 7171 2070 8

Beautiful
GALWAY
Connemara & The Burren

Gill and Macmillan

Even those who know little of Ireland, its fascinations and attractions, have heard of Galway Bay. No doubt this is largely due to the famous song. And the sun going down on Galway Bay is, indeed, a remarkable sight.

The wide expanse of the waters, fringed to north and south by the rising hills of Connacht, reflect the red glare of the dying sun with eye-straining brilliance. But the waters of the Bay are not always kind. The rugged shores have claimed a daunting share of shipwrecks over the centuries, including the shattered remnants of the Spanish Armada.

Into the head of the Bay flows the Corrib River, and on its first crossing point stands Galway City. Traditionally rich from the wine trade with Spain, Galway has always been a maritime base; indeed, for many years the Mayor of Galway was automatically an admiral charged with patrolling the western approaches to Ireland, but that task ended last century. The magnificent mace and regalia of the mayor-admiral, however, remain, as does the rigid, 18th-century layout of central Galway. But it is not only the past which makes its presence felt forcefully in Galway City. A massive, domed cathedral completed in 1965 towers over the Corrib as testimony to the Catholic faith of the inhabitants.

For socialising it is difficult to beat Galway, particularly in August and September. In the former month, the Galway Races attract the superb horses of Ireland to compete for such prestigious trophies as the Galway Plate and the Galway Hurdle, both among the most highly prized by any trainer. September sees Galway immerse itself in the Oyster Festival. Founded on the legendary quality of the seafood from Galway Bay, the festival has gained worldwide renown. The climax of events is an oyster-opening contest in which chefs from around the world compete. Of rather more interest to the layman, however, are the huge quantities of shellfish on offer in the bars and restaurants of the city.

Reaching out around Galway Bay, west of Galway City, are the embracing arms of land which form Connemara, the wild and beautiful area which has enchanted visitors for generations.

On the southern shore of Galway Bay, in County Clare, lies the unique landscape of The Burren, a treasure house of historic ruins. Caherconnel is only the largest of several massive, stone ring forts which dominate the uplands of The Burren. Built around A.D. 750, by which time the political power of the region was on the wane, Caherconnell is one of the later ring forts. Other stone forts on The Burren speak of both the prosperity and warlike disposition of the former inhabitants, and tucked just below the highlands is Dunguaire Castle, a fine fortified house of a type which became popular among petty landowners during the turbulent 15th century.

However, the true glory of The Burren is not just its history, but its flora, which is unique. The limestone and shale that form the hills have given the soil a peculiar characteristic which only certain species can tolerate. Combined with this is an exceptionally mild and wet climate due to the Gulf Stream which sweeps just offshore. Orchids are among the most prolific wild flowers on The Burren, and the botanic interest is heightened by the presence of Mediterranean, alpine and arctic plants jostling each other for roothold among the rocks. Exactly how the seeds of maidenhair fern, blue gentian, birdsfoot trefoil, cranesbill and a host of saxifrages all came to lodge and grow in The Burren is a mystery, but however it came about the result is spectacular, especially in late spring when the bulk of species flower.

The limestone of The Burren has created another marvel, this time beneath the ground. Rainwater seeping through the porous rocks has carved out extensive cave systems, some accessible only to experienced potholers, but a few of which can be explored by the less expert. The most famous are the Aillwee Caves, where organised tours may visit the spectacular rock formations of the two-million-year-old caverns. Subterranean water of quite a different kind is to be found at Liscannor, where there is a spring sacred to St Brigid, which attracts many devout pilgrims.

North of Galway Bay spreads the majestic landscape of Connemara. Arguably the finest scenic area in Ireland, Connemara has achieved much-deserved fame. The beauty of the land is matched by the rural lifestyle of the population, both being a result of the poor and infertile soils which cover the uplands. Much of the best of Connemara is enclosed within Connemara National Park, which spreads around the conical summits of the Twelve Bens.

Most people come to Connemara to enjoy the scenery, and certainly the best way to do that is on foot. But the beauty of Connemara can be treacherous. Even in the midst of the hottest summer the mountain tracks are damp underfoot. Mist and rain can close down with little notice, making it easy to stray into the dangerous bogs of the area. Despite this risk, Connemara exerts its fascination, and the beauty is undeniable.

The turbulent waters of Galway Bay have for centuries been the focus of this area of Connacht. With the alluring attractions of The Burren, Connemara and Galway City added to the glory of the Bay itself, it is no wonder that Galway Bay has become immortalised in song. Nor any wonder that those who choose to explore the beauty behind the song find all their dreams fulfilled.

Left and overleaf: The mountain-locked inlet of Killary Harbour, one of the grandest pieces of coastal scenery in County Galway.

Top left and left: Coastal scenes around Tully Cross, County Galway. **Above and overleaf:** Killary Harbour near its head at Leenane. Some 40 feet beneath the water surface the bottom is almost flat, with secure holding ground, making Killary one of the best natural anchorages in Ireland.

These pages: The Gaeltacht of County Galway embodies for many people the rural face of old Ireland. Indeed, traditional rural scenes such as these can still be found in the more remote regions, but mechanisation is increasingly gaining a hold.

Right and overleaf: Kylemore Abbey, on the shores of Kylemore Lough, stands north of the Twelve Bens. The Abbey is the Victorian creation, based on Tudor designs, of Mitchell Henry, a rich northern English merchant. Henry drained extensive areas of lakeside bog for his famous gardens.

Above and right: The Connemara coast near Clifden, one of the larger towns in the area. **Top right:** Kingstown Bay, where the Galway coast pushes furthest out into the Atlantic Ocean.

Left: The market town of Clifden, in western Galway. In the early autumn, thousands flock here for the annual Connemara Pony Show, and the town remains popular year round as a convenient place from which to explore the Connemara countryside. A short distance away is the bog in which Alcock and Brown crashed after their historic, non-stop flight across the Atlantic Ocean in 1919.

Top left: The view west from Kingstown Bay. **Left:** Sunset at
Clifden Bay. **Above:** A choppy sea off Slyne Head, arguably the
westernmost island of Connemara. **Overleaf:** A tiny, whitewashed
village on Kingstown Bay.

Right and overleaf: Scenery around the charming fishing village of Roundstone, the largest settlement for some miles in any direction. The region offers fine beaches and hill-walking, and is very popular with tourists.

Above: A boat dragged ashore beside one of the many small lakes that lie scattered around Glinsk, near the Galway border with Roscommon. **Top right:** Bertraghboy Bay, near Roundstone. **Right:** Roundstone Harbour.

Left: A tranquil sea at Carna, centre of the lucrative Galway lobster fishing industry, which sells its catch to the finest restaurants of Ireland and beyond. A festival of the local arts and traditional farming skills provides an attraction here for tourists in July.

Left: The peaks of Connemara National Park. **Above:** The Twelve Bens, the most dramatic mountains of western Galway, seen through the haze over Clifden Bay. **Overleaf:** Dawn on the Twelve Bens.

Left: The turbulent Owenriff River of County Galway, which runs down to the north shore of Galway Bay near Knock, a small village whose name drives from the Gaelic for 'the hill'. This is a tiny village tucked between the Knocknalee Hills and the sea, not the Knock of pilgrimage fame, which is situated in County Mayo.

Above: Ballynahinch Lake, which lies at the foot of the Twelve Bens. **Right:** A raging stream drops down from Bengower to Ballynahinch Lake. **Overleaf:** Derryclare Lake.

Left and overleaf: Lough Corrib, which measures 27 miles in length and is fringed to the north by numerous caves. **Above:** The Maumturk Mountains, which peak at over 2,100 feet and form a long ridge from Killary Harbour to Lough Corrib.

Facing page and right: The remote island fortress of Dunguaire Castle, in Kinvarra Bay, which has been recently restored as a private residence.
Below: A scene in Kinvarra town, on the south shore of Galway Bay.
Overleaf: An aerial view of Kinvarra.

Above: Galway Cathedral, built during the 1960s and a rather controversial addition to the city. **Right:** Galway University, built in 1849 in the style of an Oxford College. **Overleaf:** The docks of Galway, an important port for six centuries.

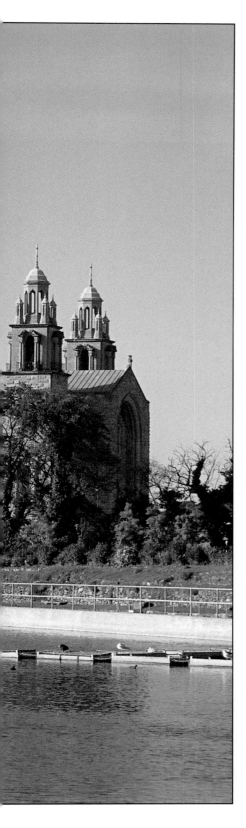

Galway City has been a place apart almost from its founding by the Norman Burgos family in the 1220s. It has long monopolised trade in this region of Connacht and has become a centre for the arts and folklore. Many of the younger generation from Dublin and the east come here for summer breaks, adding to a youthful community based around the university and its lively social life.

These pages: The Galway Races, which take place on the Ballybrit Racecourse, half-an-hour's brisk walk from the city. The races offer a strange mix of local country folk and Ireland's high society among the spectators.

Above: The Spanish Arch in Galway, where merchant ships carrying the profitable trade in Spanish wine berthed. **Top right:** Fishermen at Salmon's Leap weir. **Right:** Salthill, the popular seaside resort which adjoins Galway.

Left and below: The stone walls of Inisheer, the smallest of the Aran Islands. **Facing page:** The town of Kilronan, on Inishmore, is perhaps the most tourist-orientated part of the Arans. **Overleaf:** The stone fortress of Dun Eoghanachta on Inishmore, built some 500 years B.C.

These pages: Scenes on Inishmaan, the middle of the Aran Islands in size and position. Less frequented by tourists, Inishmaan preserves more of the unique cultural heritage of these islands on the edge of Europe.

Left: Bare limestone pavements on The Burren. The porous nature of the limestone and the chemicals which leach from it add their qualities to the stunning flora of the region.

Right: The Poulnabrone dolmen on The Burren of County Clare. These remnants of prehistoric burial grounds lie scattered over the region and argue for a sizeable population at the time of their construction.

These pages: The Burren landscapes are dominated by bare rock and open skies. Where plants can get a roothold, they tend to be a remarkable collection of alpine and arctic species found together nowhere else.

Above: The Burren. **Top right:** A thatched cottage near the town of Ballyvaughan, where many visitors stay to explore The Burren. **Right:** A canal lock at Lisdoonvarna, famous throughout Ireland as a spa town. **Overleaf:** The lake-dotted scenery of County Clare. **Last page:** The Poulnabrone dolmen.

To Vicki
Thank you ?
horsey ad?
support
Happy hack?
with love
Ceri
x

ENGLAND *on* HORSEBACK

ENGLAND *on* HORSEBACK

Zara Colchester and Charlotte Sainsbury-Plaice

Photography by Charlie Sainsbury-Plaice

CLEARVIEW

Published in the UK in 2012 by Clearview Books
11 Grosvenor Crescent, London SW1X 7EE

Cover and book design by Bernard Higton
Edited by Robin Gurdon
Maps created by Susannah English

A CIP catalogue record for this book is available from the
British Library

ISBN 978-1908337146

Printed in Singapore

Safety note:
For these rides we always wore riding hats, though we did
choose to remove them from time to time for the benefit of the
photographs. For safety's sake, please ensure that when on
horseback you always wear a riding hat.

CONTENTS

FOREWORD
BY JEREMY IRONS

Every day we immerse ourselves in a torrent of pixellated images
and polymorphous information delivered by technologies of dizzying
sophistication. We search the sky above for signs of something that
might tell us who we are, while glittering satellites spin by, faithfully
relaying our babble. Yet before the great mysteries of life we remain
as baffled as ever.

Life seems to have become inordinately complicated as we
struggle to make our way. And yet there is a remedy that has never
failed me or thousands like me.

Make your way into the open air, offer up the pores of your skin
to the rain and the sun, feel the wind in the roots of your hair and
watch as the shadows of the clouds move across the face of our
Earth. And, just maybe, peace might creep into your soul.

Best of all, if you can, get out on horseback. Being at one with an
animal can be the beginning of being at one with all things, as
indeed, at our best, we recognise ourselves to be.

The English countryside is some of the very finest in the world,
and its preservation has always been very dear to my heart.

As a celebration of that countryside and of our partnership with
a fellow creature that has put up with us for thousands of years,
I heartily recommend the pages that follow. Man and Horse in a
landscape of our own, and God's, creation.

INTRODUCTION

Approaching Guiting Manor,
Gloucestershire.

This book is about discovering the romance of the English countryside
through the relationship between man, his environment and his horse, a
relationship that has existed throughout history. It is also about the
astonishing beauty and diversity of the countryside, the network of
bridleways and byways that are a unique heritage of this country and
challenging the perception of modern Britain as a once beautiful land
largely ruined by urbanisation.

   Over the last two years we have ridden all over England from the south
coast of Dorset to the Yorkshire Moors. Our journey has taken us along
ancient drovers routes, green lanes and bridleways whose origins date back
a thousand years. We have ridden on tracks that are carefully catalogued in
the Domesday Book. Our rides have taken us past Thomas Hardy's cottage
and great stately houses, through Cotswolds villages and along beaches. We
have taken the bridle paths Anne Boleyn followed on her way to the Tower,
crossed beech woods where Henry V hunted and stopped at cottages where
Elizabeth I spent the night.

No hour of life is wasted that is spent in the saddle

Winston Churchill

The countryside of Samuel Palmer and John Keats is as alive today as it was two hundred years ago. Farmers work the land; cottagers tend their gardens. Life continues as it always has. But, the English countryside is not a museum. It has changed in the 21st century, and is under threat. Across the country people have been and are campaigning vigorously to recognise and maintain our incomparable network of rights of way. Farmers are now

being encouraged to become more environmentally aware reversing the mistakes made in the post-war period from the intensifying of production to the inefficient Common Agricultural Policy. The needs of the soil, promotion of natural habitats, public access and preservation of wild life are all now considered when grants are allocated. These policies are beginning to bring results: on our rides we now see newly planted glades, pollen and nectar strips, wildlife verges, coppicing and fresh laid hedges.

Riding towards Durdle Door on the Dorset coast.

Experiencing these positive changes on horseback not only serves to rekindle our deep connection with the landscape, but reinforces the relationship between man and horse which is as old as the hills and romantic as the countryside itself. The partnership with the horse is not about domination or power, but about trust. The elation of charging though fresh air, with the sensation of being alive and at one with an animal who will never be totally subordinate to your will justifies all one's passion. Hardy dreamed about his wife riding on Beeny Cliff: 'O the opal and the sapphire of that wandering western sea / And the woman riding high above…' Alfred Noyes wrote poems about a highwayman, wearing tight black breeches and riding 'up to the old inn door' and John Wayne crossed America on a horse in a homage to 'how the West was won.' To travel on a horse is to live in the moment. The human race's long partnership with the horse is entwined in the annals of history: it is wonderful to continue to live it.

There is a long tradition of writers who have focused on ridng through England. The Swiss equestrian explorer A.F. Tschiffely wrote in *Bridle Paths*: 'To see England properly, I recommend viewing it from the saddle, for the smell and creaking of leather and the company of a horse give it an atmosphere imaginative people can today only find in old novels.'

Crossing the farmland of north-west Norfolk.

From horseback, it seems that so little has changed. The miracle of these ancient bridle paths is that they still exist. On them, you find yourself alone, at one with countryside and your horse, feeling the essence of what rural life is about.

Indeed as we have ridden through England, we have found the landscape to be like a settled argument. A patchwork of woods and fields fought over for thousands of years, is now minutely documented in title deeds enshrined in the law of equity agreed on by generations of just and careful people, our forefathers, who have fought and died for the inalienable rights of individuals. Their care has extended to the land itself, for the hedgerows and trees we pass have all been planted and maintained in a great cooperative effort. The consensus has hardly ever been articulated but seems to us to be expressed: the Garden of England.

There are more than a million acres of common land in England and Wales. No other country in the world has this extraordinary feature. The land has remained largely undisturbed since medieval times when people relied on the commons for their survival. These acres and the bridleways and footpaths are a wonderful expression of a truly liberal society, putting the common rights of way above the interests of wealthy landowners or corporations.

The landscape of England gives one a deep message of hope. Each day we may be reminded of the degradations of the human race on our environment and images of collapsing burning trees and polluted rivers fill our screens and our hearts with despair. The woods and fields and little streams through which we ride are here to remind the world not only how it is, but how it might always be.

THE GREAT
ESTATES

This was our first ride of the year. The weather in England is never predictable, but in late March it is especially volatile and the forecast was rain. As the rides for this book are journeys through seasons as well as landscapes, we packed our wet-weather gear but, although the sky was grey and overcast, the primroses and daffodils were out and the fields were full of lambs – spring was in the air and bringing with it a feeling of optimism.

It's said that the best way to see the world is from horseback and this is certainly true of England. Being able to peer over walls and hedges into otherwise unseen worlds gives you a unique perspective of the countryside.

For this trip we'd planned a fifty-mile, circular route starting from Rendcomb near Cirencester, an elegant village which feels more French than English, where we spent the night.

Having access to this magnificent parkland we cantered along the Broad Rise.

Day 1 – Rendcomb to Miserden (16.5 miles)

The morning's ride took us through picturesque, cream-coloured, Cotswold
villages towards Cirencester Park. Owned by the Earl of Bathurst, he very
generously allows horse riding anywhere on his parkland, the only rules: no
galloping, no picnicking and a curfew of 5pm. Allen Bathurst designed the
park in 1714. Apparently, until a month before his death at the age of 91 the
old Earl would ride for at least two hours a day galloping up and down the
wide grass pathways.

   This magnificent and beautiful parkland, we soon discovered, was in
reality a labyrinth of radiating avenues, eccentric follies, huge tracks and
five-mile gallops which all looked identical. Alone in this massive park many
riders must have become seriously lost and wondered if they would make
the 5pm curfew. Our route, known as The Broad Ride, led us five miles

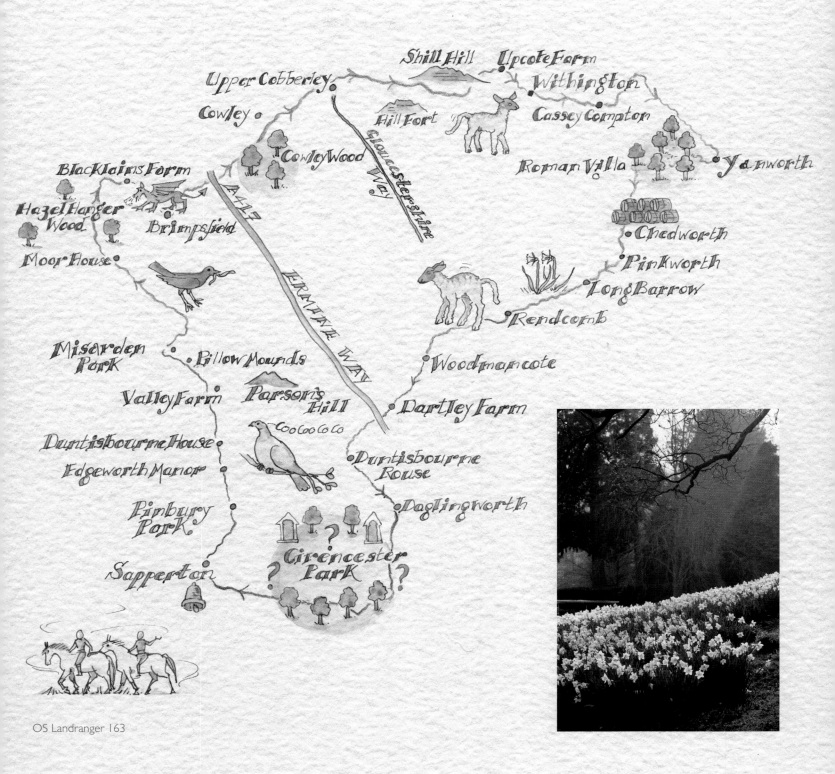

Shill Hill

Upcote Farm

Withington

Upper Cobberley

Cowley

Hill Fort

Cassey Compton

Cowley Wood

Gloucestershire Way

Roman Villa

Yanworth

Black Jains Farm

A417

Hazel Hanger Wood

Brimpsfield

Chedworth

Moor House

Pinkworth

Long Barrow

ERMINE WAY

Rendcomb

Miserden Park

Pillow Mounds

Woodmancote

Valley Farm

Parson's Hill

Coo Coo Co Co

Dartley Farm

Duntisbourne House

Edgeworth Manor

Duntisbourne Rouse

Daglingworth

Pinbury Park

Cirencester Park

?

?

?

?

Sapperton

OS Landranger 163

along a green avenue that seemed to stretch to the horizon. After passing a pair of enormous stone sentry boxes respectfully referred to as the 'Horse-Guards' we eventually ended up at a clearing known as Ten Rides Star. As the name would suggest this was a grass circle with ten identical twelve-foot wide grass tracks all radiating off. We studied our map… which route should we take? Clearly you needed a degree in navigation to get out of this park alive. What made it more challenging was the majority of the avenues led to locked gates. An hour or so later, after taking a series of wrong turns, we eventually emerged from the maze and the park, already tired and grumpy.

Our lunch stop, The Bell at Sapperton, was a honey-coloured stone pub on the edge of Cirencester Park. There were tie-up rails with a lovely old wooden sign saying 'horses'. The landlord even provided buckets of water. Clearly, we were the last in a long line of riders who had been lost in the park and found respite in the Bell Inn.

After lunch our route took us along a series of old tracks lined with beech trees stretching up to the sky like a gothic cathedral. The only sound was the crunching of the leaves under the horses' hooves. Along the way we noticed small clusters of violets and yellow primroses, we heard the coo of wood pigeon and the lyrical call of the blackbird.

The countryside opened up into the parkland of Pinbury, an imposing Jacobean house sitting in a bowl of rolling green countryside, framed by oak woods. An ancient yew hedge and a magnificent grey stone Cotswold wall wrapped themselves around the front of the house, the only barrier between the bridleway we were riding along and the garden.

Leaving Pinbury behind we rode through metalled gates up a daffodil-lined driveway towards Edgeworth Manor. We checked the map, but we were right: the bridleway again led us right past the house. All over the country there are bridleways and footpaths that go directly through people's private property, close to their homes and through their gardens. Over the

Left: Losing our way in the park led us to discover that many of the avenues led to locked gates.

Right: Taking a moment to stop and admire the beautiful Pinbury Park in the distance.

Below, right: Edgeworth Manor looms above us through the trees.

years this magic network of rights of way have survived. These ancient tracks seem to be a true manifestation of a most elemental right: the freedom for all to enjoy the beautiful countryside.

Our route over Duntisbourne Common led to more magnificent woods and up to the top of an escarpment. We stopped the horses and observed the view in silence. Below us were panoramic views of rolling green parkland, interspersed with lakes, and ancient woods of beech and oak.

By the time we arrived in the early evening at the Old Rectory in Miserden village, where we were to stay for the night, we were tired, cold and wet. Melissa Kennedy and her husband Hamish gave us a warm welcome and a cup of tea. After seeing the horses to their field, we had a bath and went down to a candlelight dinner of homemade wild garlic soup followed by a local beef stew. Over dinner we discussed our propose route. The Wills family we learned, like the Bathursts had today, owned most of the countryside we would be riding over for the next day or so.

Day 2 – Miserden to Withington (20 miles)

Our morning ride took us deep into the leafy lost world of Miserden Park. A
heavily wooded valley filled with ancient lakes, water pools and wild flowers.
Like something out of Narnia it has a gothic quality. A green cathedral of
trees reached to the sky; it is more forest than wood. In 1361 it was
rumoured the Black Prince courted the Fair Maid of Kent by one of the
lakes. As you wind your way along thin stony tracks alongside misty lakes
you imagine King Arthur's sword emerging from the murky waters. It had
started to rain, increasing the eerie atmosphere of the place. For the next

Left: The modern world receded as we made our way through the mysterious and hidden world of Miserden Park.

Right: As the evening drew in we were lost and still miles from our destination.

Left: We emerged from Miserden Park to the vivid colours of spring.

three hours we found ourselves alone in this timeless fairyland. Access to the forest by any other means than horse or foot is forbidden.

After a few hours we finally emerged from the wood and found ourselves back into the 21st century. But even romantics need food and we were hungry so stopped at the Green Dragon pub for a ploughman's lunch.

We anticipated the afternoon ride to the farm where we planned to spend the night would take no more than two hours but even so we decided to shorten the route by cutting out a large section that took us north over the main road. Everything was on track until what we had seen on the map as a bridlepath turned out to be a footpath. Creeping along the edge of a field and trying to keep out of eyeshot of the farmer, we hoped that the footpath would eventually become a bridle path. It did not. By now it was 7.30 and getting dark. There were no houses, no roads, and no people to ask for help. It looked as if we might have to spend the night in a field, holding the horses. After an hour of riding around in circles and trying unsuccessfully to

Our overnight stop was Upcote, a wonderfully
old-fashioned, working farm.

make sense of the map, we headed downhill, into a wood, ominously marked
'Private Property: Keep Out'. The gate at the bottom of the wood onto the
road was by a miracle, not locked. We spotted the lights of a house in the
distance and trotted up the drive. The surprised farmer explained we were
miles from our destination. By now it was 8.30pm and pitch black. Luckily
he was sympathetic. Our horses were put out in a small paddock with the
rams and chickens and the amused farmer kindly drove us over to our
original destination.

Upcote Farm, a magical old-fashioned farmhouse up a dirt track, is the
home of Sheila and John Platt. Sheila breeds sheep dogs and the farmyard is
like a wildlife sanctuary filled with every conceivable duck, goose and
chicken. After dinner we fell into bed, relieved not to be freezing and
bickering on some windswept escarpment overlooking Cheltenham, only to
wake up at 5am to the incredible bleating of baby lambs in the field outside
our bedroom window.

The sun began to shine as we made our way through Yanworth.

Day 3 – Withington to Rendcomb (13.5 miles)

Black rain clouds hung ominously above, so we were relieved to be riding the short distance back to Rendcomb. After a delicious breakfast of eggs and bacon we headed off up the Coln Valley. Our route took us through the picturesque village of Compton Abdale where we stopped by a fountain and allowed the horses to drink. The high point of the morning, however, was passing the romantic manor house Cassey Compton with its far-reaching views of the valley and river behind it. We rode on up to the beautiful hamlet of Yanworth where most of the houses are painted green to show their feudal allegiance to the nearby Stowell Park owned by the Vestey family.

After lunch at the Seven Tuns in Chedworth our ride was short and relaxing. By 4pm we were back at Rendcomb and loading the horses into the lorry. We had come to the end of our first journey.

Driving home along the busy A44 trunk road towards Cheltenham it struck us what a narrow reality our modern world is. For three days we had been riding through great swathes of private land, much of which has been owned by the same families for generations. These landowners often play an important role in preserving and protecting the countryside. The peace and quiet that we had experienced riding through these estates was a wonderful reminder that it is still possible to find tranquillity in this bustling overcrowded island of ours.

In Gloucestershire different things take precedence.

Above: 'I can pull faces too!'

Left: The picturesque village of Yanworth.

Overleaf: Peering over the walls of Cassey Compton, a romantic Elizabethan manor.

NORTH-WEST NORFOLK

The crisp unfolding of a brand new Ordnance Survey map holds with it the instant promise of adventure, a treasure map spread out on the kitchen table. Our first impression of 'OL 132 North West Norfolk' was the wide uncluttered space, largely free of contours and other topological indicators. Just a few villages are connected by an evenly spaced tracery of roads and tracks that criss-cross the smooth surface to the pale blue and yellow at the top of the page where the North Sea meets that land.

Norfolk may not be mountainous, wild and rugged but it is verdant, varied and coastal and we were lucky enough to be riding a large circular sweep of it. Sandringham, Massingham, Snoring, Walsingham, Hindringham, Minque and Creake – the county may be flat, but the names are full of rhyming, tongue-twisting contours, lovingly embraced by the broad Norfolk dialect. Our first stop, however, was to be a farm at the rather ordinary-sounding Harpley near King's Lynn.

The horses were unloaded and staggered stiffly down the ramp into the flint stables long ago vacated by the working animals of the old farm while we enjoyed drinks by the fire before heading out to the Rose and Crown, the village pub, for our supper.

Enjoying the waves at Holkham Beach.

Day 1 – Houghton Hall to Burnham Thorpe (16 miles)

The next morning the air was clear and noticeably nippy. Despite the sunshine Norfolk is cold. The winds come in uninterrupted off the North Sea and chill the bones. We walked to the stables down a lane frothy with ladies lace, a treasured national weed so reminiscent of the beautiful month of May. Murphy and Picasso stood, heads over stable doors, content, as if they had been in residence for years.

The first day can best be described as flowing and gentle. Our ride took us past the carefully preserved white tenants cottages and huge wrought iron gates of Houghton Hall, just outside Harpley, the birthplace and ancestral home of Sir Robert Walpole, Britain's first Prime Minister. Famous for its magnificent Palladian exterior and deer park it is just one of the large estates that bejewel the county.

The Norfolk bridleways, or 'rupps' as they are known, are sandy, deep, numerous and often lined with canopies of beech trees. The blossom of elderflower, hawthorn and cow parsley billowed white and powdery, causing the horses to snort and sneeze.

The old lanes, or rupps as they are known, were abundant with the blossom of wild flowers and the sound of birdsong.

Tranquility is assured in Norfolk, but with its steady skyline you need to concentrate on your map to make sure you don't drift down an unconnected path leading nowhere. In the old days once a track became impassable due to mud and ruts they just created a new one. This now accounts for the abundance of paths and byways all leading to the same place! We were swept along the rupps as if on a conveyor, surrounded by huge fields of potatoes, barley, wheat and maize with the occasional slice of common land and scrub along the way.

After an hour or so we reached Syderstone Common. Made up from sand, gravel and overlying chalk it is dominated by gorse and purple moor grass while the numerous pools provide ideal conditions for colonies of Natterjack Toads. Norfolk is famed for its abundance of wildlife. Seen only rarely elsewhere

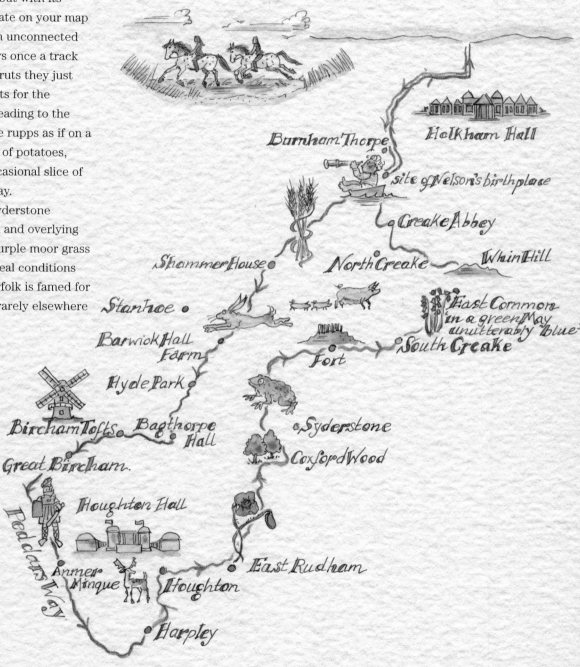

Holkham Hall

Burnham Thorpe

site of Nelson's birthplace

Creake Abbey

North Creake

Whin Hill

Shammer House

East Common
in a green May
unutterably blue

Stanhoe

South Creake

Barwick Hall Farm

Fort

Hyde Park

Syderstone

Bircham Tofts

Bagthorpe Hall

Coxford Wood

Great Bircham

Houghton Hall

Peddars Way

East Rudham

Anmer

Minque

Houghton

Harpley

OS Landranger 132

in the country hares can be found here in abundance running across the
open fields – one even jumped out from under the horse's hooves before
racing off towards the skyline.

   Remarkably that day we covered sixteen miles of country without
opening a single gate. This distinguished Norfolk from many of our other
rides. With huge fields of crops and little livestock – except for the pigs,
invariably found rooting 'free-range' inside electric-fenced paddocks – there
is little need for enclosures. Generations of farmers removed miles of
Norfolk's hedgerows in the decades after the Second World War so that now
few people remember the patchwork quilt that was the old Norfolk. Instead
it is largely a county of great open spaces.

The light flickered through the
tall trees as we rode through a
wood carpeted with campions

No better place to stop
for a picnic than in a
cool glade among the
wild flowers.

We stopped for a picnic lunch in East Common Wood and as if by a
miracle the bluebells were out bringing to mind John Masefield's poem:

How paint it: how describe? None has the power.
It only has the power upon the soul
To consecrate the spirit and the hour.
A miracle unspeakable of flower
In a green May unutterably blue

After lunch we rode through the atmospheric ruins of Creake Abbey,
statuesque against the skyline. Dismounting, we explored the small
Augustinian priory founded in 1206 as an overnight stop for pilgrims on

Top, left: A perfect example of the rich, fertile farmland that runs up to Norfolk's coast.

Bottom, left: Riding past the great Horatio Nelson's birthplace and over the stream that he would have known so well.

NORTH-WEST NORFOLK   33

their way to the shrine of Our Lady at Walsingham. Partially burnt down in 1484, the remaining monks were killed off by the plague just before the Dissolution at the end of the 1530s.

On the outskirts of the pretty village of Burnham Thorpe, we passed the birthplace of Admiral Horatio Nelson and crossed the stream where he played as a child. Unfortunately his house is no longer there but little else in the village has changed.

At about six we arrived at Whitehall Farm, home to Barry and Valerie Southerland. Tenants of the Holkham Estate, they have cleverly and wisely diversified into equestrian B and B. Great efforts have been made to devise a bridle route from the farm to the sea and we planned to try it out the following morning.

Over dinner Barry told us how Thomas Coke, Holkham's innovative owner in the mid 1700's, transformed vast areas of heath into farmland by spreading the rich underlying marl over the sandy topsoil. His novel farming techniques for converting barren land into fertile and productive fields spread far and wide across the county and his influence on farming still commands respect today.

Peering over the hedge into the ruins of Creake Abbey while riding in the quiet afternoon.

DAY 2 – Burnham Thorpe to Harpley (18 miles)

In the damp hush of sunrise the next morning we tacked up the horses and headed off down the sandy tracks toward the beach. The roads were empty and there was no one around. The paths lead us out onto 'Lady Anne's Drive' and on through the pinewoods to the glory of Holkham Beach. Once on this magnificent expanse of sand, voted the best beach in England, we discovered to our joy that we were completely alone, and even more surprisingly that horses are allowed along the vast stretch of it.

It is a heady combination: the vista of sand and sea, the gently private glow of the early morning and a horse to share it with. Murphy loved it, thrilled and trembling on sight of the ocean. Picasso was initially rather more tentative, snorting at the incoming waves and startling away from the water between his legs. Then with gentle assurance he relaxed and quite literally threw himself into the sea content to canter through the deeps. You could sense the horse's pleasure and excitement.

Our lunch stop at Bircham
Windmill.

We had such fun revisiting our childhoods as we galloped up and down the beach through the waves with not a soul in sight. After an hour or so the odd dog walker started to arrive and we retraced our steps inland. With 18 miles ahead of us it was to be a long day.

Mid-morning took us along grassy two wheeled tracks to Great Bircham, a traditional village of mellow flint cottages situated on the fringe of the Sandringham Estate. It is the site of four Bronze Age barrows. Excavated a few years ago, the contents had survived intact and a skull, funerary urns, gold and bronze pins as well as a few other small objects were found.

We stopped for lunch at Bircham Mill. Built in 1846 it, like the other great flour mills of the area, eventually fell into disuse and disrepair. It was restored it to its former glory in the 1970s and today it is one of only a handful of working windmills in the country.

After lunch, we headed towards Harpley Common via the Peddars Way, a Roman road built in AD61 soon after the Romans put down Queen Boudicca's revolt. All around us in the fields on both sides of the Peddars Way were about 50 pits from which marl – the magic ingredient Thomas Coke spread on fields to improve their fertility – was dug. Now all that remains is the odd clump of trees or bushes to mark past excavations.

Norfolk is a difficult place to get to. But once you are there it is easy riding country. The great open landscape; flint villages, tranquil soft-hewn lanes are easily accessed via the network of numerous bridleways. But what makes Norfolk truly exceptional is being allowed to ride on one of the most beautiful beaches in the world.

Galloping across Holkham's deserted sand that morning, with the waves crashing under our horses' hooves and the fluorescent early morning light glowing through pine trees was and will always be, one of our most memorable moments.

'In riding a horse we borrow freedom' –
Helen Thompson

EXMOOR

Exmoor is a world of its own. A plateau of rolling pasture, windswept moorland, panoramic sea views, ancient forests, and deep river valleys. A secret and ancient landscape that is loved by the people who live in it with a passion that is unusual in the transient Britain of today. Britain's smallest national park, Exmoor was one of the original ten created in 1949 to protect the natural beauty, wildlife and cultural heritage of the most beautiful and unspoilt parts of the country.

The Celts, Romans, Saxons and Normans all settled on Exmoor. Rounded Bronze Age barrows mark the high moorland which is crossed by even more ancient Stone Age tracks. During the medieval period the land was cultivated and new settlements established when it also became a royal hunting ground known as the Exmoor Forest. Today it retains something of the feeling of a privileged sporting preserve: many of the population are involved in the time-honoured rituals of the chase. This is a world of beaten-up Land Rovers and old tweed coats.

We had chosen to ride Charlie and Star on our two-day circular route and they emerged from their cramped five-hour journey with characteristic good nature and enthusiasm for adventure. Our first night was spent in in the picturesque village of Exford, the headquarters for the Devon and Somerset Stag Hunt, and the horsiest village in a horsey part of the country.

Riding down from the summit of Dunkery Beacon we looked out over the moors to the sea.

Roadway Lane · Wootton Courtney · Brockwell · MACMILLAN WAY · Dunster · Dunkery Beacon · Timberscombe · Bats Fort · Rodhuish · Chapel · Exeford · Wheddon Cross · Cutcombe Cross · Type Hill · Monkham · Kingsbridge · Pooltown · River Exe · Withypool

OS Landranger 181

Top, left: Approaching the ancient burial site of Dunkery Beacon at 1,700 ft.

Bottom, left: Both horses and riders enjoyed the panoramic views from the Herepath.

DAY 1 – Dunkery Hill to Rodhuish (21 miles)

We began the first day's ride by climbing straight up onto to Dunkery Hill, a magnificent remote expanse of moorland. Much of Exmoor is inaccessible by car and no roads or buildings blight this landscape, instead groups of wild ponies with their foals graze the windswept heath-covered slopes. Exmoor ponies are the most ancient breeds we have in Britain and have probably run wild since before the last ice Age. The ghosts of history, whether they be ancient burial sites, old beech hedges, pack horse tracks, or Celtic place names, serve as a constant reminder that here the past is always with us.

Riding on along an ancient grassy track, known as the Herepath, we eventually came to the summit at Dunkery Beacon. At 1,705 feet above sea level it is the highest place on Exmoor. Sitting on our horses on the top of a Bronze Age barrow, we looked out at the staggering views across the moors, northwards towards to the Bristol Channel and south across central Devon to Dartmoor. Common land, heaths and open down land are all too rare in heavily populated southern England. Luckily this magnificent coastal moorland will remain protected forever by the National Trust. Looking out over the moor to the sea beyond it struck us how wild and remote Exmoor must have seemed to the Saxons and the Normans a thousand years ago.

From Dunkery Hill we descended a steep stony track until eventually we reached Brockwell and the village of Wootton Courtenay. From there onwards our route took us along Roadway Lane, a track that is a good example of an ancient hollow lane or 'holloway'. These narrow paths have been used for over 1,000 years and have been constantly eroded by centuries of use by packhorses. It is said that every one hundred years they become two foot deeper.

Bridle signs on Exmoor are quite unique: natural wood posts only about 3'6 high. The National Parks Authority are reluctant to install bridle signs in some areas, particularly on moorland, because they feel that they detract from the wild nature of the environment which might help explain why we managed to get lost so often during our ride! Another unique feature of Exmoor is its high hedges on top of earth banks. Some are extremely old, dating back to the Saxon or medieval times when they were used to define parish boundaries. Dozens of miles of beech hedge perched on stone walls were planted to provide shelter for the animals in winter. It seems a miracle they thrive, for the soil of the moor is acid and not theoretically suitable for beech.

Following The Macmillan Way the next section took us along the top of Wooton Common Ridge where we could see Minehead and the sea below before we turned deep, deep into the woods. Over 17,000 acres of woodland were planted, mainly between 1921 and 1924, and evergreens such as Douglas fir and larch dominate. Row upon row of dark green conifers ensure that no wild flowers, animals or birds can make the wood their home.

Right: Cautiously picking our way down the ancient Holloway, through the emerald green light of early summer.

Left, and opposite: Charlie, the enthusiastic traveller, enjoyed his temporary home in the stableyard at Higher Rodhuish Farm.

The 13th-century chapel at Rodhuish.

Because every stony track looks the same it is extremely easy to take the wrong turning in these looming woods and get lost for many hours. We were exhausted and irritable when we finally emerged, but our lovely horses, who had done all the hard work, were as game as ever.

Finally reaching Rodhuish for the night we found ourselves outside a beautiful 14th century farmhouse. The Thomas family have farmed Higher Rodhuish Farm for over a hundred years. Of the area's four main farms, three have been in the same family since the nineteenth century. Over a delicious dinner, we learnt more about farm life from Alan and his brother, Peter. Growing up in the late fifties most people had never travelled further than the nearest small town in their entire lives, and few of them could read or write more than their names. Having no electricity, there was no TV to fill the evenings, instead people walked to each other's houses. Oil lamps in winter, no running water, no heating. 'In the winter you would wake up and there would be ice on the inside of the windows. In all weathers, until it was dark, people were outside. Children walked to school and back. It was a real community, everyone knew everyone else. The stables were full of carthorses. There would have been six full time workers on the farm all hedging and ditching.' When Jennifer married Alan in 1967 the farm

labourers were paid £9 week and the village had two blacksmiths and a butcher. All the farm workers had a cottage and a patch of land to grow vegetables. The shepherd, Jim, lived within 50 yards of this farmhouse all of his life. There was a sense of place of belonging: 'It's the old families that made Exmoor…but they were the farming families not the aristocrats. ' According to Alan the farmers started the hunting on Exmoor as a reaction to smart local hunts who would not allow them in. By his own admission Exmoor is a closed society, families marry other Exmoor families. 'Peter was the clever one. Managed to get away didn't you. Went to university and then travelled the world. Lives in Guildford and teaches graduates'. But it was Peter who revelled in the stories of the past.

The next morning we were taken to see St. Bartholomew's, a white 13th century chapel in Rodhuish. Jennifer and other locals in the community, including the writer Penelope Lively, had raised funds and managed to restore this simple chapel.

The endless streams and rivers of Exmoor gave the horses ample opportunities for refreshment

DAY 2 – Rodhuish to Exford (19 miles)

After a hearty breakfast and a sad farewell, we set off up Monkham and Lype Hill and then on over undulating countryside to Cutcombe. Mentioned in the Domesday Book it has an 11th-century church. Our pub stop was the aptly named The Rest and be Thankful at Wheddon Cross.

After crossing the River Exe and the Winsford valley, home to the largest and best know herds of Exmoor ponies, we followed our route back to Exford. Tired after our twenty-mile ride we decided to stay one more night.

You cannot visit Exmoor without stopping off at the Royal Oak in Withypool. Famous for three hundred years, this pub is homage to fox and stag hunting. The dark interior, with its oak beamed ceiling, is adorned with photographs of past (Hunt) masters. On the far wall by the open fire is an old glass cabinet filled with hunting buttons from all over the country. The Royal Oak makes no concessions to the 21st century – there is no bleached pine or taupe paint here. When we arrived the pub was almost empty. Two elderly men, in old tweed coats, were propping up the bar and talking to the barman, Jake. They hardly acknowledged us, just giving us a glance as if to say 'we don't know you' as we sat down for our meal.

In Exmoor there is a saying that it takes five years before you get spoken to, ten years to be accepted and twenty-five years before you are local. Despite the fact there is no mobile signal, that driving snow can coat the heather in May, that the windswept moors are often blanketed for days by mist and fog, people who live on Exmoor would not live anywhere else.

'The wind of heaven is that
which blows between a horses
ears' – Arabian proverb

HARDY'S DORSET

Dorset is the county of Hardy, where he grew up and where he wrote his greatest poems and books. Much of the landscape and many of the towns and villages that he described so passionately can still be identified, so riding through the countryside that he knew and loved so deeply is a moving experience. Often, as we travelled we would recognize a landmark or a place from a novel. Sometimes riding along an ancient track we would remind ourselves that this was a route along which Hardy would have walked. He saw beauty and value in simple rural life, and his message is as important today as it was one hundred and fifty years ago.

It was midsummer and the weather was warm as we guided the lorry through pretty narrow lanes to Buckland Newton near Dorchester where we were to be spending the first night. Later that evening, having turned the horses out into a large field, we sat down with Jenny Needham and her husband and enjoyed a delicious dinner of home-reared lamb washed down with generous amounts of red wine.

'There is nothing so good for the inside of a man as the outside of a horse' – Lord Palmerston

DAY 1 – Buckland Newton to Okeford Fitzpaine (13 miles)

Riding up the Wessex Ridgeway in the footsteps of our ancestors.

We set off uphill on an old track, grooved by centuries of horse-drawn carts. The views in the distance were of undulating small fields and ancient woodland of coppiced oaks and ash. We rode along in a dreamy ambience of dappled light, cow parsley, honeysuckle, foxglove and birdsong towards the Dorset Gap, an isolated green and leafy crossway deep in the woods. at times bending low to avoid over-hanging branches. This is an ancient crossroads, through which the Exeter to Salisbury pack-route once passed. Today it is a haven for wildlife. We stopped and dismounted to write a message in the notebook that contains the thoughts and names of people who have walked or ridden by over the years which is kept in a small box near the track. Now finding our way out of this secret hideaway turned out to be something of a challenge.

Wild flowers surrounded us throughout our ride.

After some wrong turns we emerged on to a steep-sided escarpment. Long pale grass rippled in the warm wind as we stopped and admired the views to Poole and Glastonbury Tor to the south. The only sound was the soft blowing of the horses' nostrils, birds of prey 'hawking' above and skylarks warding us off their ground-built nests. We followed the old path

Okeford Fitzpaine

Ibberton

Wessex Ridgeway

Rawlsbury Camp

Buckland Newton

Dorset Gap

Winterborne Stickland

Plush

A354

Fishmore Hill Farm

Piddlehinton

Dole's Hill

Dewlish

Milborne St Andrew

Winterborne Kingston

Ridgeway

Hardy's Cottage

Left: Making our way up to Bulbarrow Hill.

Top, right: Looking out over Dorset from the ancient hillfort of Rawlsbury Camp.

Bottom, right: Cutting through the young corn.

along the ridge and through what can only be described as a kissing gate for horses – it was quite dangerous and uncharacteristic as the bridleways here were generally well marked and accessible.

Riding on through farms and pastureland we climbed the Wessex Ridgeway up to Rawlsbury Camp, a magnificent Iron Age hill fort at the top of Bulbarrow Hill. As the horses picked their way up and down the extraordinary contours of the fort you could only guess at the layers of history that lay beneath their hooves. It is easy to see why our Iron Age ancestors built here, the views are panoramic.

Our route took us on towards Wooland and Ibberton Hill. To the west were amazing views of the Blackmore Vale and its infamous hedges, so revered by the hunting fraternity. The sky emerging blue again behind clouds, hanging high above the valley.

A gateway on the side of a narrow country lane provided a good spot for a picnic. No more than 1 or 2 cars passed by during the hour. The horses had learned to graze from their long tie-ups without getting their legs entwined with the rope – we just ate and dozed in the sun.

After lunch we began to encounter larger arable fields rippling with ripening barley, wheat and beans. Often, the bridleways struck a straight,

clear path through the centre of the crops. We crossed shallow fords and made our way through villages, with their thatch and timber-framed brick houses straggling along narrow lanes and unkempt verges. Turning back onto the Wessex Ridgeway we eventually dropped down into the Forestry Commission land at Okeford Hill which, like many others of its type, has become a dark and dense forest – the oaks, ash and beech trees of the ancient wood cut down and replaced by silent and seemingly lifeless conifers.

A day of wide-reaching views over the county ended with a climb down the smooth contours of Okeford Hill in the quiet evening sunlight – it is rumored fairies can be seen dancing there at midnight – to Okeford Fitzpaine and the fields and hospitality of Louly Thornycroft, our hostess for the night

DAY 2 – Okeford Fitzpaine to Milton Abbas (21 miles)

After a good look at the maps we said our farewells setting off through the centre of Okeford Fitzpaine, past the church and cottages, and back up Okeford Hill. The morning's ride took us up over the northern scarp of the chalk hills, with wonderful views over the Blackmore Vale. This landscape is dominated by open fields of arable crops, with wide verges which gave us plenty of opportunity to canter. The bridleways were varied in their upkeep; some narrow and overgrown, others with generous clearings.

Crossing the main road to Winterborne Kingston was slightly dicey, but once across we found ourselves on the old Roman road that ran from Dorchester and Salisbury, our route taking us along valleys and streams to the beautiful and timeless village of Dewlish. We rode by a dairy herd ambling to their pasture in the soft evening light, nudging and licking the stockman who had stopped to patiently guide us in the right direction with his gentle Dorset burr. Our destination, Fishmore Hill Farm, is brilliantly equipped for horses and situated in an exceptional location, perched above billowing green wheat fields that stretch out towards the horizon. Sarah Clark, our hostess is an expert equestrian host and offers advice on day rides and longer routes from the farm. We ate at the pub and turned in early, twenty one miles of riding (with the odd diversion due to dodgy map reading) had tired us out.

Above, right: 'A canter is a cure for every evil' – Benjamin Disraeli.

Right: Horses graze on the open downland against a threatening sky.

A unique glimpse of Thomas Hardy's cottage at Higher Bockhampton.

DAY 3 Milton Abbas to West Lulworth (20 miles)

The morning took us into the heart of Hardy country. His cottage at Higher Bockhampton is only a four-mile diversion from the twenty-mile route we had mapped out, along a bridleway that takes you right up to the cottage. Built by his great-grandfather in 1800 this is where Hardy grew up and little has changed. It is also where he wrote many of his masterpieces though sadly most of the surrounding heath that inspired him is gone, having been planted with the all too familiar conifers. Sitting on our horses we were able to look over the old stone wall into the cottage garden which Hardy must have known so well. An unforgettable moment.

Back on track after our detour, we traversed the remote chalk country of central Dorset towards Piddlehampton and Doles Hill. Our lunch stop was the Brace of Feathers in Plush, a small and isolated village nestled at the head of a valley in the shelter of the surrounding hills. The pub is everything you would expect a Dorset pub should be – authentically old fashioned and serving delicious food. It was now only a short distance back to Buckland Newton where we had began our journey three days earlier but it felt too magical to return home just yet. Instead we decided to box the horses and drive them to the coast. We had been told about a wonderful small farmhouse that would put us up for the night which turned out to be surrounded by rolling arable fields and soft green down land reaching right to the edge of the cliffs high on a windswept hill above West Lulworth.

Approaching our lunch stop, The Brace of Feathers at Plush –
the quintessential English pub.

Riding down
to the coast at
Durdle Door.

DAY 4 – The Coast (5 miles)

Early the next morning, we rode out of the farm onto a narrow track that
took us high up onto the cliffs overlooking Durdle Door where the views out
to sea were staggering. The horses snorted nervously as they looked over
the cliff edge at the waves booming onto the rocks far below. This is a
dramatic landscape, thrilling to experience on the back of a horse.

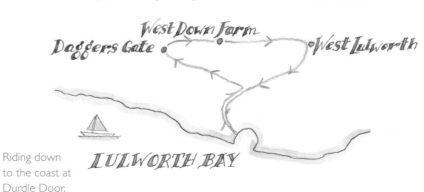

Looking across to Durdle Door, the inspiration for many scenes in Hardy's *Far from the Madding Crowd*, from the high grassland above.

We had been given special permission to ride directly down to the sea so we headed off across the cliffs and down to Lulworth Cove, a perfect, moon-shaped bay with a small shingle beach. This is Dorset's coastline at its most picturesque. Riding down the slippery stone ramp and into the shallow water of the harbour we found ourselves cantering through the waves amongst the colourful array of fishing boats working or drawn up on the sand. The fishermen pulling in the morning catch seemed totally unfazed as we plunged in and out of the sea on our horses.

Invigorated, we made our way back up the valley towards Daggers Gate and West Down Farm. Our four-day trip had come to an end and it was finally time to pack up and head off North.

Much of Dorset still looks like it did when Hardy wrote about it. Of course some of the county has suffered from forestry and modern farming but it is not all doom and gloom. Riding for four days made us appreciate that where the thickets, hedgerows and old meadows remain the little valleys and steep-sided dales are as beautiful as they have ever been.

Splashing around with friends through the shallows in Lulworth Cove.

THE VALE OF BELVOIR

The Vale of Belvoir is home to one of England's most romantic and magical castles. Sitting high on an escarpment Belvoir Castle, almost always visible on the horizon, seemed to follow us – just as the Eiffel Tower does in Paris – while we rode for two days through the countryside around it. The name Belvoir means 'beautiful view' and the castle occupies a commanding position with breath-taking panoramas across wide swathes of farmland. The present castle is the fourth to have stood on the site since the Norman times. Lived in by the Manners family for eight hundred years the castle was first built by their ancestor, Robert de Todeni, standard-bearer for William the Conqueror, soon after the Conquest. The native Anglo-Saxon population, unable to pronounce the foreign name, called it 'Beaver' and it is still pronounced this way today.

Our first night was spent at Sewstern Grange a lovely old farmhouse filled with hunting prints, where we had supper in a cosy parlour surrounded by dogs.

'When you are on a great horse you will have the best seat you will ever have.' – Winston Churchill

DAY 1 – Sewstern to Belvoir Castle (16.5 miles)

The village of Sewstern grew up alongside an ancient salt route known as Sewstern Lane. It was one of the road's few overnight stopping places and would have had at least one inn and a medieval church, which has long since disappeared. The village became a backwater after Sewstern Lane was abandoned as a coaching route.

Ancient salt routes criss-crossed the British Isles transporting one of the ancient world's necessities inland from the few centres of production on the seacoasts and tidal rivers. This particular lane is probably at least 4,000 years old, dating from the Bronze Age. Running for many miles along the Leicestershire-Lincolnshire border it was in use for all traffic until the end of the 17th century, when it was abandoned in favour of the Great North Road, probably because Sewstern was the only overnight stop for 40 miles. Also known as The Drift, Sewstern Lane later became a recognized route by which cattle from Scotland and the north of England reached the Midlands and London. Traditionally in the 18th century the cattle-drovers continued

Riding along Sewstern Lane, an ancient salt-trading route that later came to be known as 'The Drift'.

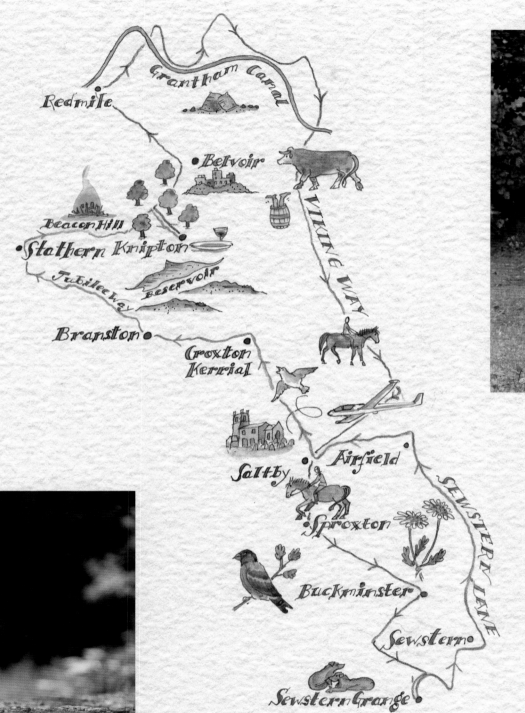

Redmile

Grantham Canal

Belvoir

VIKING WAY

Beacon Hill

Stathern Knipton

Jubilee Way

Reservoir

Branston

Croxton Kerrial

Saltby

Airfield

SEWSTERN LANE

Sproxton

Buckminster

Sewstern

Sewstern Grange

OS Landranger 129 and 130

to use this track in preference to the Great North Road, on which they would have had to pay taxes, and they were happy to sleep on the roadside alongside their animals.

After the middle of the nineteenth century the emerging railway network took on the task of transporting animals and the drovers' lanes fell into disuse. Today, Sewstern Lane is magically quiet, flanked by fields of red poppies and white daisies. Bluetits, bullfinches, wrens, sparrows and starlings busily flew around us and we even heard a skylark trilling high above our heads. Drovers' roads always avoided towns and so make for some of the nicest walking and riding routes in the country. The section that we rode along is also part of the 'Viking Way', a long-distance path that runs for 120 miles across Lincolnshire from the Humber estuary to Rutland.

The next stretch of bridleway was somewhat hazardous as we passed alongside Saltby Airfield, a gliding club where planes with towing cables are constantly taking off, circling and landing as they launch the gliders high into the sky. Our route took us north towards Branston and the Jubilee Way (another recent name) which we followed for the next couple of miles

We paused for a moment to pay our respects at the Saltby Airfield war memorial.

before a track led us a mile into a wood and then out onto Beacon Hill, the highest point in Leicestershire. Amazingly there is a stone memorial on the site to the beacon that was lit in 1588 as part of a nationwide chain to warn people of the arrival of the Spanish Armada.

Our route then took us north through Branston towards Stathern on the Jubilee Way. After following a track through Barkestone Wood we rode down a small lane into the village of Knipton where we were to spend the night in the Manners Arms. That night we enjoyed a delicious dinner of wild venison before collapsing into bed.

Above: The old salt road was bordered for mile after mile by drifts of daisies.

Left: Opening another of the endless gates, Zara on Picasso.

DAY 2 Belvoir Castle to Sewstern (22 miles)

The fairly-tale castle loomed over us as we retraced our steps back to
Terrace Hills into Old Park Wood. This gothic fantasy was built after
chapters of sackings and fires in the nineteenth century and could easily
pass for Hogworts, Harry Potter's fictional school. The parkland and gardens
are inspiring, and there is no doubt that the presence of the great ducal seat
is felt everywhere in the Vale of Belvoir.

The early part of the day's ride took us through Redmile and on over the
Grantham Canal. Opened in 1739, it transported agricultural produce to
Nottingham and coal back to the countryside before falling into disuse when
the railway was built alongside it. Crossing the canal we got more fantastic
views of Belvoir Castle in the warm morning haze before heading on towards
Easthorpe along a series of grassy tracks that passed through a patchwork
of small fields.

To have a break from the heat of the day we stopped for a drink at The
Rutland Arms outside the village of Woolsthorpe. The pub, better known as
'Bobby Taylor's Famous Dirty Duck' for some reason we were not able to
fathom, is next to the canal so we were able to able to relax by the

Top left: The waterside was lined with beautiful rushes and
wild flowers.

Above: As we crossed the Grantham Canal for a much-needed drink at the 'Dirty Duck' we were still in sight of Belvoir Castle.

waterside and enjoy yet more views of the castle. Passing over the water once more we followed a narrow grassy track past the gates of the castle and the Brewer's grave – supposedly the last resting place of a brewer from Belvoir Castle who drowned in a barrel of beer! – which now also marks the end of the Jubilee Way.

Turning south onto the Viking Way and once more onto Sewstern Lane, we headed on across cultivated fields and through some gates towards Sproxton, passing by St Bartholomew's church standing alone outside the village. This church dates from the 12th century and the churchyard contains some of the best-preserved Anglo Saxon crosses in England.

At the junction in Sproxton we followed the road that runs between Colsterworth and Melton Mowbray. The town is famous not just for its pork pies but also as the epicentre of the hunting world. The Cottesmore, the Quorn and the Belvoir all meet around it as it forms the junction of their country. Many famous people, including royalty, have hunted over this

Many ancient trading routes criss-cross what are the country's most famous hunting fields.

Fields of poppies and wildflowers are plentiful here in early summer.

country for the last two hundred years. The expression 'paint the town red' comes from Melton Mowbray when one of the hunts celebrates after a successful kill. And Belvoir, of course, is also famous for its hunt – the hounds have been kenneled at the castle since 1809. They are one of very few remaining packs of purebred Old English foxhounds in the United Kingdom; and this type of foxhound is distinctive for its black and tan colour. That afternoon, as we rode back over this famous hunt country towards Sewstern Grange it was easy to visualize generations of upper class 'thrusters' decked out in their red hunting jackets careening across these hills and vales.

Our pace, however, was more sedate. Being on horseback and ambling through the summer countryside seemed to us the summit of privilege. For us this was no adrenalin rush but an opportunity to be at one with a beautiful animal in a beautiful place. The sense of harmony you achieve with a horse you have ridden up hill and down dale through the days is never to be forgotten.

THE WELSH BORDERS

The wildest and most remote of all our rides crossed the Welsh Marches, land that was fought over for well over a thousand years and is strewn with the ruins of castles that had their days of battle and bloodshed. Names like Owen Glyndwr, Jack Mytton, Llewellyn and King Offa resonate in the history that shaped this turbulent and romantic countryside.

For two days our route took us over hills covered with heather, bracken and gorse with nothing but the scream of the buzzard and native, short-limbed Radnor sheep for company. The upland moors – one of the few great wildernesses we have left in this country – stretch out into infinity with nothing but the odd sagging barn or tumbledown cottage to break the view. This is a land of water: meandering streams and clear bubbling brooks remind one of the generous showers blown in from the Irish Sea.

We hardly saw another person – unlike the Brecon Beacons or the Black Mountains, there are no tourists here – and with no noise from traffic or aeroplanes the silence is real. These rolling hills give a feeling of eternity, of timelessness, a knowledge of the fact that this landscape will be here long after we are gone.

Here there are no distractions and the modern world does not trespass.

OS Landranger 163

The isolated house at Fron Farm where we started our ride.

For the intrepid rider, the Welsh Borders is perfect riding country. However, it is not for the faint-hearted. There are no way posts or clearly marked bridleways, no-one to ask directions and no gourmet pubs to escape the rain at lunchtime. You need a compass to navigate the mossy sheep tracks that crisscross the hills and are perfect for galloping but also easy to get lost on. If the weather changes, which it can do very quickly, the mist can come down and it is extremely easy for even the most experienced rider to lose all sense of place.

We started our ride at Fron Farm, an isolated farmhouse perched high on the edge of Beacon Hill. The only way to reach it is to follow a four-mile, rutted track uphill through two working farms where sheepdogs run out barking as you drive through yards littered with old tractors and machinery. The 16th century stone farmhouse, owned by Chris and Judy Menges, was a wreck when they moved from London thirty years ago but has been lovingly restored over the years and is a testimony to their understanding of Welsh vernacular architecture. Later, with a glass of white wine, we sat outside in the warm summer's evening watching the sun vanish over the distant hills.

DAY 1 – Beacon Hill to Cwmllechwedd Fawr (16.5 miles)

We woke up to a beautiful sunny day, with blue skies and not a cloud in sight. Riding from the farm took us directly out onto Beacon Hill, a vast expanse of high common land owned by the Crown Estate. Here bracken-covered hills fold into one another for mile upon mile with little or no landmarks other than the odd small clump of trees. It was not long before we were lost, and bickering. The bracken was so high that it was impossible to see any bridle gate or way marker. Trying not to become too tetchy we checked the maps and the compass and retraced our steps. Luckily, after a few wrong starts we eventually found ourselves heading over the upper slopes of Beacon Hill and northwards where we crossed the River Teme into Shropshire. Stopping to give the horses a well-deserved drink, we stood looking out ahead towards the romantically named Llanfair Hill in the distance.

Back on the horses, we followed an old drove track for a mile or so until eventually we reached the Jack Mytton Way. This long-distance bridleway commemorates 'Mad Jack' Mytton, a notorious early 19th century Shropshire squire. A wildly enthusiastic huntsman, he was reputed to have bought his horse into the dining room and given it so much red wine it died. Alcoholic and spendthrift, he led a totally dissipated life and gambled away his fortune, dying in debtors prison at the age of 38. Even so, his tireless exploration of the country he loved has earned him immortality

The Jack Mytton Way runs for a spell alongside the celebrated Offa's Dyke. Built by King Offa in the eighth century as a boundary between Wales and England, the dyke is an amazing hundred and sixty-mile earth mound. Much of Offa's Dyke is now a footpath but there was no evidence that anyone had ever set foot on this stretch.

Above: Between the areas of open moorland we crossed lush pastures in the lowland hills.

Above right: Man and horse: a story as old as the hills we were riding across.

Right: A moment to reflect on our journey as we rested at the top of Pool Hill.

Following the faint track we eventually reached a high plateau overlooking the moorland below, known as Pool Hill. Sitting quietly whilst our horses grazed, we admired the panoramic views stretching out below us. This was a wonderful moment: alone in this vast open space, with the purple hills, the perfect blue sky and the silence.

On Pool Hill we picked up the track marked Owen Glyndwr's Way. A hugely romantic figure, Owen Glyndwr fought long and bitterly for the Welsh cause against the English from 1380–1405 and became the national hero. Although his rising was brutally repressed, he was never defeated and died a free man. The Owen Glyndwr Way is now a National track that takes you meandering for 160 miles all over the Welsh Borders. The route took us off Pool Hill and towards Stankey Hill. The grassy track was soft and inviting and soon we were galloping flat out with the warm wind blowing in our

faces. Finally the track petered out and after fording a stream and
continuing through fields and valleys we eventually came to Cwmllechwedd
Fawr, the farm of the 'two Johns' where we were staying the night.

Originally from London they moved to the area about twenty years ago
and still love the secrecy and isolation of the Welsh Borders. Whilst one
John looks after the farm, breeding Welsh blacks, the other sings in operas
all over the world. That night we had a delicious dinner. All the food had
been grown in the garden. It was like dining in a five star London restaurant.
Exhausted we collapsed into our lovely beds.

The following morning, we awoke to another beautiful warm day,
breakfast was all ready and the table laid with fresh orange juice, organic
eggs from the hens and home-reared bacon. The full rural idyll… but over
breakfast the conversation turned to the imminent threat from wind
turbines. Shockingly, we learnt that the the very country we had been riding
over the day before had been earmarked to be covered by a massive wind
farm – madness!

..

Above: Approaching
Cwmllechwedd Fawr,
where we spent the
night, across the rolling
meadows.

Right and top right:
A series of old tracks
and gateways led us
ever deeper into this
remote country.

DAY 2 – Cwmllechwedd Fawr to Beacon Hill (14 miles)

Saying a fond farewell to the two Johns we set off once again into the wilderness, retracing our steps until we reached the hidden cottage of Bwlch Gwyn. A narrow and stony track then led us northwards and up onto Black Mountain. By now we had left the Owen Glyndwr Way well behind us and had to rely on old way marks, many of which had either fallen down or disappeared completely. A series of old tracks led us on and up over the wild and remote common. As we reached the brow of the hill we caught sight of an elderly man with wild hair and a young boy. They were the first people we had seen all day. Presuming the man must be a local farmer we stopped our horses to ask if we were on the right track. The boy looked at us rather suspiciously: clearly visitors were a rare event in these remote parts.

We headed off towards a place intriguingly marked on the map as 'New Invention'. In reality it consisted of a few abandoned sheep hurdles lying in a field but from there we rode down into a steep valley alongside a small bubbling stream. After fording the stream and clambering up the steep bank

The Owen Glyndwr Way. This remote and romantic track winds its way like a ribbon through a wilderness steeped in the history of the Welsh Borders.

a narrow sheep track eventually lead us into a mysterious hidden valley, marked as Upper Cwm-yr-Ingel on the map, with a stream running through and a derelict old white cottage. Our ride through the beautiful and unspoilt landscape had already been a revelation but nothing could have prepared us for the pure magic of Upper Cwm-yr-Ingel. There is something almost spiritual in the beauty and simplicity of this place. Hidden from the world, with no road or track to it, it is as perfect a place as anywhere on earth.

The last part of our ride took us back over the wilds of Beacon Hill. Hopelessly lost again! Eventually an overgrown path led us directly back to the Fron and Judy Menges, who was waiting for us with an amused smile on her face. We will not be the last people to get lost on Beacon Hill.

After a well-needed cup of tea and some home-made cake we boxed up our horses and hit the road. Or the road hit us. The shock of the bustling, ugly modern world after the lonely wild uplands made us reflect on how precious it is.

As we dropped down to the end of our ride we were surrounded by the flowers of early summer.

CRANBORNE CHASE

Known as the 'wheat basket of England', Cranborne Chase lies across the hills of Dorset, the plains of Wiltshire and the moorland of the New Forest. Once a royal hunting reserve, the rolling chalk grassland, huge hedgeless fields, ancient woodlands and shallow valleys give this area its unique and recognizable character. Roman roads and drover's tracks form the backbone of the bridleways that make Cranborne Chase such wonderful riding country.

We arrived at Boveridge Farm near the village of Cranborne in the middle of summer, the busiest time of year, so the barns were full of recently harvested grain and stacked with straw bales. Our hostess, Tina Yarrow, was in the garden pulling up weeds and tending borders – despite running the farm she is one of those capable people who still miraculously seems to have time to keep her garden looking beautiful!

From our bedroom window the views were impressive. Massive fields of wheat, barley and oats leave one under no illusion. Farming here is big business.

Riding through the open prairies of Cranborne Chase on a midsummer's day.

DAY 1 – Cranborne to Sutton Mandeville (15 miles)

Tina – who alongside running the farm and a racehorse livery, is also master of the Portman Hunt – and her daughter, Lucinda, were able to join us on the first leg of the ride. Throwing caution to the wind we asked Tina to direct us to the first road crossing even though this would mean deviating from the map so we rode on for an hour or so through arable fields interspersed with gorse pasture and wild flowers. Looking down into the valley below us we could see the tents and teepees of 'Endorse it in Dorset', a local music festival that takes place every year. Faint melodies of music caught the wind.

At this point Tina turned around and headed home whilst we continued on. We soon discovered however that we were lost and nothing on our map seemed to correspond to where we were. Retracing our steps we eventually found ourselves riding into the quiet village of Pentridge, often referred to as the 'gateway to Dorset'. Pentridge's flint and peachy brick cottages hide

Left: Everywhere we rode we were surrounded by acres of dusty, dry ears of wheat.

The flint walls of the Dorset villages are as familiar to the area as the expanses of cornfields.

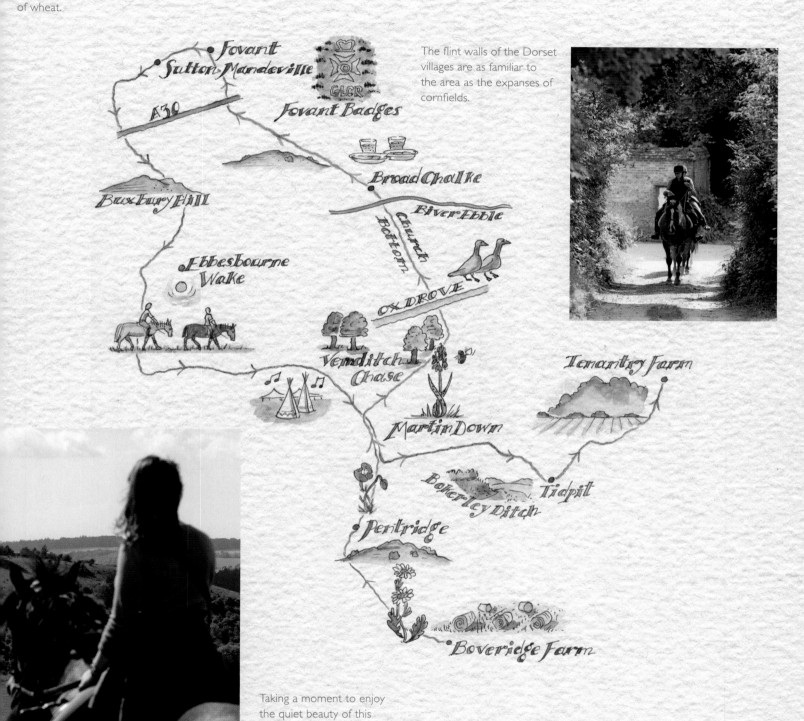

Fovant
Sutton Mandeville
A30
Fovant Badges
GLCR

Broad Chalke

Buxbury Hill

River Ebble

Church Bottom

Ebbesbourne Wake

OX DROVE

Verditch Chase

Tenantry Farm

Martin Down

Pentridge

Bokerley Ditch

Tidpit

Boveridge Farm

Taking a moment to enjoy the quiet beauty of this ancient countryside.

OS Landranger 184 and 195

behind crumbling walls bordered by hollyhocks and roses. This is
quintessential England.

Relieved to be back on track, we rode into an open area known as Martin
Down, crossing the ancient rampart of Bokerley Dyke. No one knows why it
was built but the local people suspect that it was intended to keep the
Saxon invaders out and for hundreds of years this area remained Saxon
free. This snake-like bank would have been an amazing engineering feat
when it was built over a thousand years ago.

Martin Down is a windswept and chalky reserve that is home to unusual
plants including various orchids, toadflax and fleawort as well as rare bats,
birds and bumblebees. We saw none of these, however, as we only had eyes
for our map until we finally found our way out through the maze of paths
and over the busy main road into the old hunting grounds of Vernditch

Above: Following the tracks of a combine harvester we made our way through a newly cut cornfield.

Chase. Originally part of Cranborne Chase, Vernditch was separated in 1630 in a feud between the Earls of Salisbury and Pembroke. Peace descended again as we passed through its grassland pastures and ancient broadleaf woods, following dusty sun-dappled tracks deep into the fairytale forest, half expecting the Earl of Pembroke on his hunter to come thundering around the corner.

Eventually we crossed the Ox Drove, a medieval drovers' road that ran from Shaftsbury to Salisbury. For hundreds of years these roads were used to transport livestock to markets and towns, many of them dating back to before the Romans. Cattle, sheep, geese, turkeys and horses were driven from one end of England to another along these ancient tracks. Cattle were fitted with iron shoes; geese and turkey's feet were tarred and sanded. A drover, whose job was to ensure that the animals reached the market place in good health, would accompany the livestock on foot or horseback. This was no easy task for the animals all had to be to fed, watered and sheltered along the way. Many of these journeys took months and were hazardous. The drover had to be on the constant lookout for thieves.

Droving declined during the nineteenth century with the coming of the railway and more intensive use of the countryside. Many of the old routes fell into disuse but although no longer used for transport they are still very much in existence and accessible to walkers or riders today.

Right: Meandering along the Oxdrove, an ancient track believed to be over 4,000 years old.

Leaving the Ox Drove we made a gentle descent through Church Bottom between the dry and dusty chalk downs to the Ebble Valley to our lunch stop in the pretty village of Broad Chalke. After lunch we climbed up in between lush hedges and along field margins enjoying wide-open views of wheat and barley fields stretching away into the distance. On reaching the ridge top we crossed the old Coach Road that runs for about 13 miles along the top of the downs between Salisbury and Shaftesbury, built high like many old drovers' routes to prevent the coaches getting stuck in the clay soil in the valley bottom.

It was early evening by now and the light was warm and incandescent with the dust of harvest. We turned off into a large field overlooking stunning views of Buxbury Hill and the Nadder Valley, our destination. To the right we could see the faint outlines of the famous regimental badges cut into the chalky side of the down by American troops stationed there in the First World War.

We wound our way downhill. Expansive views of the harvest below, the scale of the fields breathtaking, the machines working the great fields like diminutive toys dotted on the landscape. We descended a leafy gully to reach the A30. Our stop, Cromwell Manor in the village of Sutton Mandeville, was situated a mile or so on the other side of the road which cut through the valley like a sharp knife.

Josie, a colorful local councillor and her husband Martin, a retired dairy farmer, welcomed us warmly. We rather regretted not having organized to stay for dinner for it would have been delicious and fun. Instead we headed to the King John in Tollard Royale.

Top, right: This is as close as you can get to the great American West in this country.

Bottom, right: Coming face to face with the reality and efficiency of modern farming.

A windowsill at Tenantry Farm.

DAY 2 – Sutton Mandeville to Rockbourne (15 miles)

Next morning after breakfast in Josie's pretty dining room we mounted up and made our way down a dark, tree-lined bridleway to Buxbury Hill. From the top we could see all the way to Salisbury Plain as well as the transforming effects of modern agriculture upon the landscape. Huge prairie-like fields stretched out into the horizon, their original contours ripped out and the new boundaries dictated by the turns of the great modern combine harvesters. Undisturbed chalk down land is usually extremely rich in

Sundappled tracks bordered by high hedgerows pass between the great cornfields.

archaeological remains but over the last fifty years, much of the countryside has been ploughed up for intensive farming. Circles of standing stones, henges, hill forts, burial chambers and other such relics of history have been lost forever.

We rode on up hills and down steep descents into the valleys below. At one point we passed through a small gate into a crop of dense game cover. It towered over us eerily but the horses took this jungle of tall vegetation in their stride and pushed their way through until we emerged to a clear view of the harvest in full swing below. Huge combines worked the sides of the valley opposite as we dropped like needles in a haystack down through the remaining standing wheat fields to the road.

Following narrow lanes lined with dense hedgerows that weaved through the valley bottom we rode past traditional brick and flint cottages, the scent of mown grass welcoming us after the exposed downs and hillsides. At midday, we found a shady glade for a picnic lunch and tethered the hot and grateful horses to the trees.

Afterwards we climbed up through some beautiful old chalk lands, late summer wild flowers hanging on beside the ancient track that zigzagged deep into the hillsides. The air was hot, silent and balmy. Pale, dry grasses grew out of the white soil, the sky bright blue above. This was England burning in the embers of late summer but it could have been central Spain.

We were then reunited with the Ox Drove, our route taking us back into Vernditch Chase where we followed Bokerley Dyke for nearly two miles to the village of Martin. The road wound on through Tidpit among gentle pastoral views of meadows and church spires and on to the long dark drive of Tenantry Farm.

An impressive tree-lined drive led us to expect a bleak and austere house but instead we came upon a modest, welcoming farmhouse, made all the more special by Ailsa and Robin Macleod who have lived on the farm for the last forty years. Harvest was in full swing and Robin was tense: rain was on

Riding through the wildflowers and grasses of the chalk downland

its way and he had another 20 acres of hay to cut. The weather forecast was terrible. The next day apparently it was supposed to tip down. As we sat at the kitchen table enjoying our cup of tea and discussing the weather, it seemed not remotely surprising that this will always be a be a particularly English pastime. Only in England can the weather be this unpredictable.

After a delicious dinner at the local pub, we collapsed into bed. Outside, the relentless din of the grain dryer whirled way in the large shed across the yard. I thought I would never sleep the noise was so loud. The following day our worst fears were confirmed and we awoke to lashing, horizontal rain. The skies were dark and the clouds loomed angry and black above us. We reflected that in all our rides we had never cancelled a day for the weather but Robin had predicted the storm and was gloomily confident it would last all day. We threw the towel in, boxed up and despondently drove home through the downpour.

THE YORKSHIRE MOORS

The Yorkshire Moors will probably forever be associated with the Brontë sisters and Wuthering Heights. Indeed at the very beginning of the novel, Mr. Lockwood arrives at the Grange in the West Riding and says: 'In all England, I do not believe that I could have fixed on a situation so completely removed from the stir of society.' The North Yorkshire Moors also remain a remote and romantic place of inspiration to writers and painters. There is a lonely timelessness to this landscape. Intensive farming has not blighted the purple heather and prickly gorse of these bracken-covered hills. This is still a remote and austere landscape where you can be at one with the natural world.

Rather than drag our horses all the way to Yorkshire we decided instead to rent from a local livery yard. Arriving for our 'assessment' we were watched with a critical eye as we tacked up the horses and tried unsuccessfully to tie a basic slipknot. Next we were asked to ride around an indoor arena. The young instructor barked instructions at us in her heavy Yorkshire accent as we trotted around in circles. After a gruelling twenty minutes we were told to pull up. I was convinced that we were to be told we were not competent enough to rent horses but it appeared we had passed the test and it was agreed that two horses would be delivered the following morning.

'One can get in a car and see what man has made. One must get on a horse to see what God has made.' – author unknown

DAY 1 – Newton-on-Rawcliffe to Harwood Dale (16 miles)

Amidst the great open spaces of Levisham Moor.

We awoke at around 8am to the sound of a lorry delivering our two horses – nice old-fashioned types, charmingly named Loulou and Comet. Setting off, the first part of the ride took us up and onto Levisham Moor, a treeless, glaciated expanse of moorland. The wind is a constant companion on these moors. In winter it sweeps in from the North Sea bringing icy conditions but even in summer the wind blew so strongly while we climbed the steep, stony track up a deep ravine we could hardly breathe. On the top, we found ourselves on a high plateau overlooking Newtondale, a spectacular iron-age gorge and the Hole of Horcum, a 400-foot deep hole a mile wide, right below us. The bleak moorland stretched out in front of us with not a bush or a tree

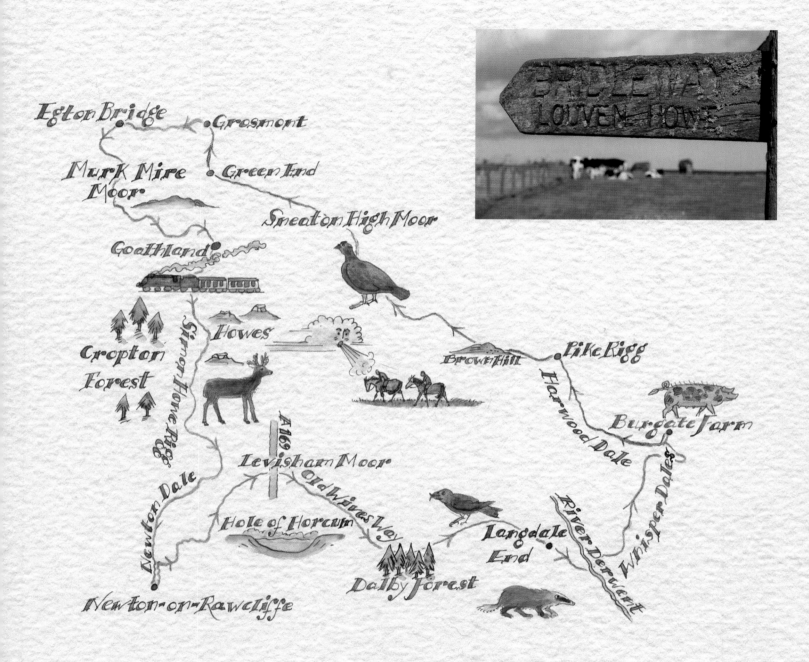

Egton Bridge
Grosmont
Murk Mire Moor
Green End
Sneaton High Moor
Goathland
Howes
Cropton Forest
Simon Howe Rigg
Brown Hill
Pike Rigg
Harwood Dale
Burgate Farm
A 169
Levisham Moor
Old Wives Way
Newton Dale
Hole of Horcum
Langdale End
River Derwent
Whisper Dales
Dalby Forest
Newton-on-Rawcliffe

in sight. This was like being in Mongolia and a sharp contrast to the soft green undulating countryside that we had encountered on so many of the previous rides.

We followed our maps carefully, sticking to a stony track that led us across the moor past the legendary Saltersgate Inn which was originally used by fish smugglers trying to avoid the salt tax. Our route then took us along the Old Wives Way towards the northern edge of Dalby Forest on the southern slopes of the North York Moors National Park where, during the 1930s, unemployed men were set to work breaking ground and building tracks in one of a number of so-called 'Instructional Centres' designed to 'harden up' unemployed young men. The forest is now home to roe deer, badgers and elusive birds like the crossbill and nightjar.

From the top of the Old Wives Way we stopped and admired the magnificent views of the moors to the north. Purple heather, bright yellow gorse and the russet hues of dying bracken moulded together to create the classic colour combination for which the moors are renowned. Continuing past the remote pub at Langdale End and workmen's cottages with red slate roofs, a sign nailed to the gate saying 'Hardstruggle Cottages'. We crossed the stepping-stones on the River Derwent into the valley of Whisperdale, and were immediately struck by the contrast in scenery that is characteristic of this area. One moment we were riding on treeless moorland, the next through a rich green glade filled with ancient beech and oaks. This contrast in the landscape is reflected in the weather. A cold wind and black clouds can be replaced in a matter of moments by blue skies and sunshine.

Above, right: Looking out over the Hole of Horcum the moors stretched away from us as far as the eye could see.

Below, right: We descended to a landscape of patchwork fields and working farms.

Crossing the stepping stones over the River Derwent.

Overleaf: 'The world is a book, and those who do not travel read only a page.' — St Augustine

The howling wind we had experienced on the top of Levisham Moor had vanished the moment we had ridden off the top of the plateau to be replaced by summer showers. Now the rain stopped and quite suddenly a beautiful rainbow appeared. It was hardy believable that something so perfect could just emerge from nowhere. The extraordinary array of colours set against the soft green fields created a moment of pure magic.

Dropping into Harwood Dale we arrived at Burgate Farm, the home of Catriona Cook, to be greeted by the honks of a large sow lying in her stall surrounded by her piglets. Cattle, pigs, geese, chickens, horses and humans all coexist together in this old-fashioned farm which the Cooks have been farming since 1972. Then there were seventeen working dairy farms but now there are only four, leaving the valley silent and just a shadow of its former self. Over dinner Catriona explained how she has spent the last forty years fighting for public access in Yorkshire and across England. She has OS maps dating back to 1830s showing the old drovers' roads and bridleways her work has reopened. Her love of long-distance riding came from her childhood when she would travel with her father from one end of the country to the other. Now in her sixties she is still fighting the good fight and is as strident as ever. 'In a hundred years time no one will remember who won Badminton but they will still have the bridleways.'

Catriona Cook's extraordinary collection of antique maps.

DAY 2 – Harwood Dale to Eskdaleside (19 miles)

The following morning we followed Catriona on her New Forest pony over Sneaton High Moor. Covered in almost black heather, this vast treeless plateau is lunar in feeling. Riding here in the bad weather could be extremely frightening as there are bogs and the mist can come down and engulf you but Catriona is not one to have ever been intimidated by such things. As we rode on she explained that much of the ancient road we were using had been left off the Definitive Map, but research and pressure had finally meant that it had been reinstated. A few hours later, at Pike Rigg junction, Catriona turned around and rode for home. As she disappeared off into the distance, a small speck on the lonely moor, we had nothing but admiration for this amazing lady. Fearless and stoical she was made of strong stuff and an inspiration to us both.

This bleak lunar landscape is broken up by the contrasting vivid green and purple hues of bog and heather.

We continued on along the deep rutted path over the moors, nervously avoiding anything that looked like a potential bog. At certain points Fylingdales Early Warning Station loomed in front of us, a grim reminder of the past and present dangers facing modern society, unexpected on these empty moors. We then followed a bridleway track to the small town of Grosmont. In front of us were spectacular views to Whitby and the sea beyond. We arrived at our destination, a bed and breakfast on the outskirts of Eskdaleside, in time for dinner.

DAY 3 – Eskdaleside to Newton-on-Rawcliffe (19 miles)

The morning's ride took us through the village of Goathland, the site of an early iron works. Today the railway still runs through and we were lucky enough to catch sight of a steam train as it chugged past. After crossing the Egon Bridge we headed south onto Murk Mire Moor following the Simon Howe Rigg directly over the moors. This huge expanse of moorland is dotted with ancient burial mounds, cairns, stone circles, standing stones, round barrows and other Bronze Age monuments. Howes are the local name for the round barrows, built as burial mounds around 1500 BC. This area of open heathland is grassy and spectacular for riding. Lady Elizabeth Kirk, Catriona's friend and mentor, had been responsible for reinstating large sections of this bridleway. Looking across the valley to the west were lines of grouse butts. This is big grouse shooting country but luckily our route was well away from the guns.

The Simon Howe Rigg led us deep into Cropton Forest. Mostly consisting of conifers planted in the 1920s using the labour force from the local disused mines. We rode on into the murky depths of the forest for an hour or more. In these dark woods you lose all sense of time and place. The track then took us out onto Newton Dale and eventually back into Newton-on-Rawcliffe where we had started our ride three days earlier.

Riding over the Yorkshire Moors is not for the faint hearted. They are bleak and in bad weather unforgiving but these wild open spaces seem to fulfill a deeply felt need in us, a psychological lifeline that connects us to who we really are and where we come from.

Opposite: Man, his environment and his horse – a relationship that has existed throughout history.

THE SURREY SUSSEX COMMONS

It is easy to have a preconceived idea of Surrey – close to London, full of busy roads with suburban houses and manicured countryside. This is the land of the stockbroker and the commuter, not the obvious venue for a riding holiday. Yet we kept hearing about a long distance ride around Surrey and Sussex, devised by Tracey Martin and her husband Richard, that sounded worth exploring. After some research, we set out on a three-day ride, escorted by Richard – it was, we were told, very easy to 'get lost' in Surrey!

After a harrowing drive in our lorry along the A3 we arrived in Rushmore where we stayed the night. Darkness had descended so it was impossible to see what the countryside outside our bedroom window looked like.

Despite it's proximity to London it is surprisingly easy to get lost in the great open spaces of Surrey.

DAY 1 - Rushmore to Blackdown (17 miles)

On our first morning, as we headed west towards Frensham Common, the feeling of suburbia soon vanished and we were to discover the wilder side of Surrey. Over the next three days we would ride across some of the most magnificent ancient commons in England. These heathlands were originally created by prehistoric farmers to graze their sheep. Bracken was cut for bedding and fuel collected from the woodland.

England has lost a great deal of its heathland in the last two hundred years but amazingly a quarter of what we do have left is in Surrey. During the enclosures of the 17th and 18th centuries when much of England was being parcelled up and laid claim to, the Surrey commons were not deemed productive enough to bother with. The nutrients in the acidic soil, known

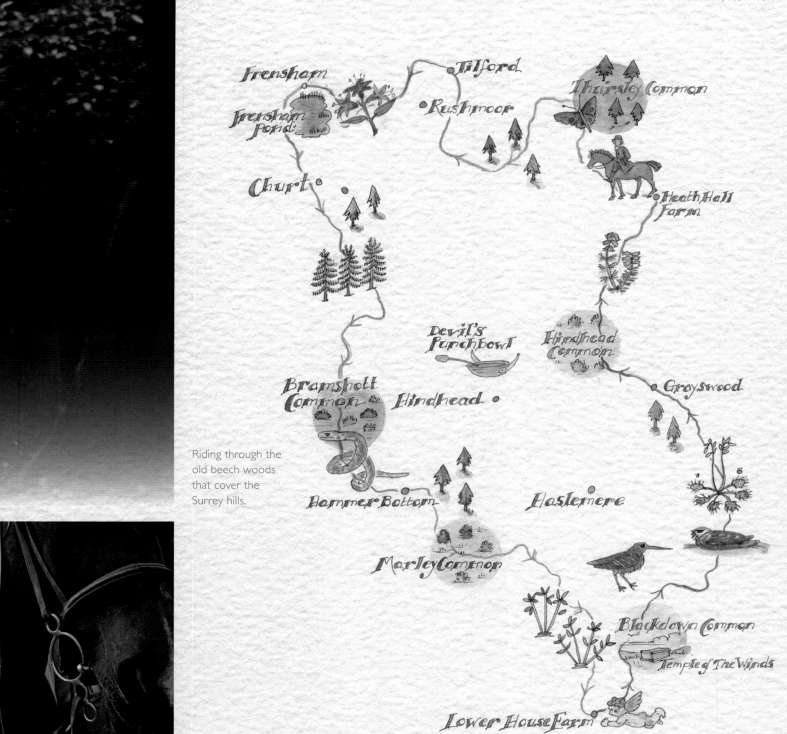

Riding through the
old beech woods
that cover the
Surrey hills.

OS Landranger 186

locally as 'green sand', were easily washed away meaning that little but heather, gorse and bracken could grow.

The result was that until the late 18th Century, despite its proximity to London, Surrey was sparsely populated and remained poor. It was the railway in the 19th Century that changed everything. People flocked out to Surrey to escape the city. Nowadays executive houses and immaculate shiny cars have taken over yet the countryside of the past has not been totally obliterated. Hidden behind the rows of expensive suburban homes are myriad small lanes that lead directly on to the commons and into ancient woods.

Heading south towards Hammer Bottom and on through some conifer plantations we reached Marley Common. Like many of the other commons we were to ride through, Marley is a large expanse of heathland interspersed with woodland and soft sandy tracks. Nothing is marked and all the tracks look exactly the same. This type of heathland supports some surprisingly rare wildlife. Over three hundred species of wild flower grow here including numerous orchids. Myriad insects, frogs, toads, newts, adders, grass snakes and lizards have all made their home here.

From Marley Common we headed south into Marley Wood and soon we were riding through ancient oaks and chestnuts. Many of the chestnuts are still being coppiced in the same way they would have been hundreds of years ago. Today the wood is used for post and rail fencing but in the past it also yielded charcoal to supply the ironworks that were a feature of this area. Ironstone was a big business in the weald of Surrey and Sussex – iron ore was smelted for cannon balls and farm machinery up until the Napoleonic wars.

As we left the woods behind us, the views to the southwest looking off towards Green Hill and Stanley Common were quite spectacular. No houses or roads could be seen, just a patchwork of green fields, woods and undulating countryside.

We had now crossed from Surrey into Sussex to reach our overnight stop. Surrounded by 500 acres, Lower House Farm is like a little jewel hidden away from the busy modern world. It is, however, no ordinary farmhouse and Nicky and John Braithwaite are no ordinary farmers. A lover of antiques and a collector of anything Italianate Nicky's father enlarged the house to house his ever-expanding and eclectic collection of antiques.

Right: The leafy lanes of suburban heaven cut through the expanse of trees.

Below: Surrey the most densely wooded area of England.

Every spare inch is packed with eccentric and priceless Italian antiques. Eight-foot Madonnas, painted wooden saints, stone altars, gilded baroque mirrors and even an enormous four poster Medici bed are crammed inside. Staying there is a surreal experience. We felt as if we had been transported to an Italian palace or onto the set of a Fellini film. Both Nicky and John are architects, and their fabulous farmhouse is a testament to their artistic and original personalities.

Day 2 – Blackdown to Thursley (10 miles)

The morning's ride took us on to Black Down Common, 965 acres of which has been designated an Area of Outstanding Natural Beauty. A combination of heathland and old woodland there is an abundance of rich fauna and flora, birds include woodcock, nightjar, crossbill and woodpeckers. The area is dominated by heather, with wetland plants such as cross-leaved heath, rough-leaved sundew and hare's tail cotton grasses. It is also the highest point in Sussex. From the top you can see across the wooded landscape to the Weald and further to the sea. A favourite haunt of the poet Alfred Lord Tennyson he built himself a small memorial, known as The Temple of the Winds, where he would sit and look out over the panoramic views.

Heading north up a bridleway along streambeds and through woods we gradually climbed up to Hindhead Common, a vast expanse of woods and lowland heath. Because it is steep and with few breaks in the trees it is extremely difficult to navigate. It is easy to become disoriented trying to follow the badly marked sandy tracks.

Like Black Down Common, Hindhead is owned and managed by the National Trust: amongst its 1,600 acres is the famous Devil's Punch Bowl, so named because the mist lies in the bowl and appears to flow over the rim as if it were boiling over. Grazing of the heathland by commoners ended around the mid-1900s, which allowed the spread of birch, pine and bracken over the heather. A programme of active reclamation is now reversing this encroachment. Exmoor ponies and highland cattle are helping to restore and maintain these areas.

Sir Robert Hunter, co-founder of the National Trust, lived in Haslemere. Shortly after forming the trust in 1895 he organized a public subscription to

The dappled light broke through the leaves onto the leaf-covered path through the woods.

Above: Gazing out from Alfred Lord Tennyson's favourite spot, 'The Temple of the Winds.'

Below: An unusual house for Surrey.

purchase much of Hindhead common. This was one of the trust's earliest acquisitions. Sir Robert's far-sightedness has meant that a century later we can still enjoy the landscape he worked so hard to save.

Some time later we followed a few small roads and tracks of the Common down to Heath Hall Farm for tea where we were to spend the third night. The Langdale family have lived there for 400 years and originally made their money from iron smelting. Over a cup of tea, we learnt that William Cobbett the famous equestrian explorer had actually stayed in the house during one of his rural rides.

That night, we borrowed two bikes and headed off to the Dog and Pheasant pub in Brook. The steep climb after dinner back up to the farmhouse was a lot more strenuous than either of us had bargained for. The countryside is surprisingly hilly and it was only now we fully appreciated how exhausted poor Picasso and Otto must be after clambering up and down slopes all day long with us on their backs.

Day 3 – Thursley to Rushmore (16 miles)

The horses seemed spritely enough the next day, however, as we set off across Thursley Common. The soft sandy paths, the gorse and the purple heather gave the common an ageless beauty. Its boggy pools and ditches support a host of rare butterflies including the Silver Studded Blue and the Purple Emperor. It is one of the richest sites for birds in southern England and one of the few areas where the Dartford warbler survives.

By now the sun had come and the temperature was climbing into the mid 80s so we stopped for lunch on a green by the river at Tilford to eat our sandwiches and relax for an hour.

The afternoon's ride took us up to Alice Holt forest. Originally an ancient oak wood it was planted with conifers in the 1920s but many of the dense rows of pines are now being cleared so wildlife can flourish. Despite all the conservation work that is going on, much of the area is still densely wooded with pine trees. Riding through the forest on a bed of soft needles with the light filtering though the tall trees gives the place an eerie Gothic feeling. The forest is dark and a little spooky – it is not surprising that this where many of the scenes from Gladiator were filmed.

By now, we had nearly completed our three-day circuit. The final lap of our journey took us back onto Frensham Common to where we had started.

Surrey had not been what we had expected. The densely populated county that you normally encounter by car does not prepare you for the extraordinary expanses of hidden common land that still exist. It felt remarkable, one could almost say miraculous, that we had been able to ride for day after day on ancient heathland dating back thousands of years. The conservation work that is going on today to protect and safeguard these wonderful stretches of wild country is inspiring, we need to ensure that they continue to be preserved for generations to come.

'A man on a horse is spiritually, as well as physically, bigger than a man on foot.' – John Steinbeck

THE SHROPSHIRE HILLS

Shropshire is a place of awe-inspiring beauty and its landscape offers the best of all worlds – soft, pastoral sophistication with wild, rolling, heather-covered hills – as well as some of the most varied riding in the country.

Our first evening was spent in Dudgeley, a farmhouse nestled into the foot of the Long Mynd, the huge prehistoric ridge which rose, brown and brooding, above us dominating the whole area, known locally as 'Little Switzerland'.

The scent of wood smoke, evocative of the late onset of autumn, that pervaded the house made it hard to believe that just two weeks previously we had been riding through a baking sand bowl on the Surrey hills. Tonight we enjoyed a sumptuous feast of wild smoked salmon with cats and dogs luxuriating by the Aga, keeping warm against the evening chill.

Over the hills and faraway – The Long Mynd rises up above the surrounding landscape.

DAY 1 – All Stretton to Stiperstones (15 miles)

The following morning we rode out into the drizzle. One of the benefits of starting from Dudgeley is that you can ride directly onto the hills. Travelling at a leisurely pace up a rise know locally as 'The Gallops' we got a hazy view of Plush Hill and Jonathan's Rock in the distance.

In good weather the views from here would undoubtedly be magnificent. But today, swirling cloud gave us only the odd glimpse of the dusky valleys below.

Following a grassy track we eventually merged with the 'Port Way', an important prehistoric track which runs across the Long Mynd. Built on the high ground to avoid the woods, valleys and steams below, this old road was once used to transport the goods for the Neolithic axe trade. Originating near Plowden in the southwest and running all the way to Shrewsbury in the north in a relatively straight line, the route was still in use during the Roman period. By the Middle Ages it was known as The King's Highway and it was not so long ago that working teams of horses pulled wagons of

Helen, our guide – known as 'Lofty Granny' – leads the way as we ride up 'the gallops' in the mist.

Snailbeach

Kennels Farm

Pulverbatch

Lordshill Baptist Chapel

Motte & Bailey

Wilderley Hall

The Hollies

Stiperstones

STIPERSTONES

Devil's Chair

GONE TO EARTH

Pickescott

BLACK DITCH

Wild Edric

Strong North Westerly

Betchcotts Hills

'bent hawthorns like crippled old men'

The Bog

Bog Hill

Plush Hill

Dudgeley Farm

'Golloping Vicar'

Robin Hood Butts

Jonathan's Rock

'The Gallops'

Bridges

PORTWAY

Shooting Box

All Stretton

Adstone Hill

Pole Bank

Medlicott

Pole Cottage

Church Stretton

Stanbatch

LONGMYND

Midland Gliding Club

Little Stretton

JACK MYTTON WAY

Minton

Priors Holt Hill

agricultural produce between the market towns of Bishops Castle and Shrewsbury, wearing down the surface so that in some places it runs well below the level of the moor. Only after the introduction of the railways did the track fall into disuse. Although somewhat neglected today, it remains a valuable reminder of our rich and varied history.

High up on the ridge a strong north-westerly wind was blowing so hard that we could hardly breathe. Here there were hawthorn trees exposed to the gales, thorny and bowing to the east like crippled old men. We discovered that Helen, our sprightly and adventurous guide, liked to go at quite a clip and our leisurely pace soon turned into more of a canter and gallop than a walk.

We stopped for a sandwich in a shelterbelt of oak trees whose trunks gnarled into the embankment of an old drovers' road, an ideal spot on this drizzly windswept day. In the afternoon our route took us along tracks which stretched and curled around hillsides frequently fringed by great growths of oak and elder. On a clear day the views of North Shropshire and the Cheshire Plain include The Wrekin and the Ironbridge Chimney, both stark reminders of Shropshire's industrial heritage.

Leaving the comfort of the lanes we ascended 'The Hollies', an eerie track named for its abundance of ancient trees which took us past a sinister old Baptist chapel perched alone on the edge of the hill. Known as Lordshill it was mentioned in Mary Webb's book 'Gone to Earth'.

A rutted track eventually lead us up to the magnificent Stiperstones – a quartzite ridge formed around 480 million years ago. Crowned by several jagged hilltops these magnificent rocks look as if they would be more at home in Arizona than Shropshire. Here the atmosphere is rich in myth and folklore. On this murky day the legend and ghost of Wild Edric, a Saxon earl who held his lands here in defiance of the Normans after 1066, felt all too real. Perhaps the horses, who seemed particularly sharp and wary also felt something.

The ridge along which we travelled runs for three miles across the top. The swirling wet mist made the craggy rocks all the more dramatic and exciting. Through the gloom we could just glimpse The Devil's Chair and

Top right: Like phantoms in the mist we rode towards the Stiperstones.

Bottom right: Through the dense fog we could glimpse The Devil's Chair and Manstone Rock.

Heading for lunch in the shelter of a belt of oak trees.

We rode on through heather-clad hills until our route, the
Portway, converged with the Jack Mytton Way.

Manstone Rock looming eerily over us a short distance away. This dramatic landscape permeates the soul and lives in one's memory long after you have left the place.

The lead industry was vital to these remote communities for many centuries. Miners living in smallholdings, grazing their livestock on the surrounding heathland. By the twentieth century mining was diminishing and although the last cottage was deserted in the 1960s we rode directly past two that have been beautifully restored in a project which aims to recreate the villages that flourished high up on The Stiperstones.

We rode on, climbing the heather clad hills, the magnificent Corndon Hill visible in the distance, until we saw Stiperstones village itself, where we were to spend the night, hiding in the folds of the valley below. In places the hillside fairly fell away, only singular surefooted sheep brave enough to tackle the slopes.

Weaving our way down from the moors towards The Bog.

We made our way down through the ferns and heather to the home of Timothy Rawdon Mogg, otherwise know as the galloping vicar. Timothy had kindly offered to house the horses for the night and ride with us next day. Having taken care of the horses, Timothy drove us to the Stiperstones Inn where we were to be spending the night. A traditional family pub with a lovely warm fire, it was a little short on bedrooms however and the five of us had been allocated two small bedrooms for the night. This somewhat eccentric arrangement did not go unnoticed by the other guests who looked at us, suspiciously wondering what our group was up to! After a delicious and jolly dinner we collapsed into our 'dormitories' and fell fast asleep.

Our second day was brighter, allowing us to canter across the green, grassy slopes.

DAY 2 – Stiperstones to All Stretton (17 miles)

The next morning we awoke to discover that the fog had lifted. Turning south east we headed back towards the Long Mynd and it was not long before once again we were galloping flat out across the green grassy slopes.

For a while we traversed the beautiful wild open country, crossing a number of gated lanes. There were sensational views below of South Shropshire carved into regular patterns, the effect of the 18th century enclosure acts. The market town of Bishops Castle could be seen in the distance against the background of the hills of the Marches, a constant visual reminder of our proximity to Wales. The views of the Welsh Hills rolled invitingly into the distance as The Portway track converged with the Jack Mytton Way. 'Mad Jack' was born in Shropshire in 1796 and his name has become synonymous with the bridleway that crosses the Welsh border with Shropshire. Called to the House of Commons as an MP he quit after only half an hour and never returned. The dull speeches, which drove Jack Mytton from Westminster, ensured he now had time to turn his life into an undying legend. It is said that he once jumped his horse over a table laid for dinner. Despite his drunken death in a debtor's prison at the age of 38, crowds lined the roads along the fifteen-mile funeral route, the church bells tolled, and every shop was closed.

A member of the Midlands Gliding Club swoops overhead.

'Horses lend us the wings
we lack.' – Pam Brown

The Galloping Vicar leads
the way across the beautiful
wild open country.

A moment as the sun baths Caer Caradoc in the evening light.

We turned into the forestry towards Priors Holt, and then on through the pretty villages of Minton and Little Stretton. Soon we were climbing steeply back again towards the summit of the Long Mynd. In places this part of the ride is positively vertiginous. Pole Bank, the highest point on The Mynd sits at nearly 1,700ft (516m) and it is worth taking a minute to study the brass plaque erected here to point out all visible mountains and hills from this spot. Sitting on our horses, looking out over the views below, I was reminded once again that we are custodians of such treasures of rural delight in this country. Whatever the woes of the past, the great political decisions that have swept away much of our rural heritage together with the individual acts that have collectively nibbled at the edges, we are lucky to still have some of the most beautiful untouched countryside in the world.

We returned across the top of the Mynd, native ponies grazing quietly as we passed by. It had been a long day and the horses, unusually tired from all the steep hills they had carried us over, were all too pleased when we finally dropped back down to the gentle pastures of Dudgeley. As we descended we were treated to a glorious view of Caer Caradoc (1,625ft, 495m) bathed in late afternoon sunshine.

We will be back, though next time we will explore the bridleways of the Shropshire peaks that inspired A.E. Housman's 'blue remembered hills.'

Heading home over the Long Mynd.

THE HEART OF ENGLAND

Rural Warwickshire offers a combination of woodland pasture, rolling green fields and prosperous market towns. Quintessentially English, much of the area's wealth was built on wool and this is reflected in the country houses and beautiful villages that are so characteristic and unique to our countryside.

We had decided to do this ride in early February and unfortunately the weather had turned. Snow was predicated for the two days we had chosen, but even though it was icy cold we were determined go ahead.

Our first night was spent in a magnificent Jacobean house, Admington Hall, whose beautiful bedrooms have real fires and huge four-poster beds. After dinner, we walked to the magnificent stone stable block to check on the horses. A dozen or so large hunters in thick rugs stood contently munching on hay nets. A profound sense of peace and calm emanated from the horses as we stood in silence savouring the moment. Later, snuggling happily under the thick layer of blankets between the crisp linen sheets, I could not help but think that Jilly Cooper would be quite impressed by this set up.

Riding up the driveway to Foxcote House on a frosty morning.

DAY 1 - Admington Hall to Norton Hall (14 miles)

Above: Admington Hall.
Below: The visitors' book at Admington.

After breakfast we headed off towards the northeast across the fields of the Admington estate. Above our heads hawks hovered high in the sky hungrily searching for their prey. The morning ride took us towards Foxcote, an imposing honey-coloured Georgian house set half way up a three-mile drive. Amazingly, the bridleway took us right past the front of the house. We stopped the horses by the gate and gazed at the house for a long moment. Surrounded by perfectly manicured green pasture, it gives one a feeling of tranquillity and peace that makes it quite exceptional. All the shutters, though, were closed and with no-one around there was stillness to the place that felt just a little bit sad. Perhaps such a beautiful place should not be left empty.

Admington Hall

Norton Hall

Mickleton

Kiftsgate
Hidcote

Ilmington

Stoke Hill

Foxcote

Burnt Norton

Windmill Hill

Dover's Hill

Ebrington

Chipping Campden

Great Western

OS Landranger 151

A cold and frosty
morning for the start
of our ride.

Passing by a magnificent yew hedge that wrapped itself around the house
we rode through a metal gate and down the drive until after another mile
we emerged out of the park and back into the real world. Continuing along a
series of bridleways we soon reached the beautiful market town of Chipping
Campden, one of the treasures of Gloucestershire. Its fine stone buildings,
its uncommonly pretty streets and its terraced houses are a legacy to the
prosperity of the medieval sheep trade. The fact that it has not been ruined
is also a testament to its successful preservation. Today it is a popular
Cotswold tourist destination. People flock from all over the world to stay in
the old inns and hotels. But despite all the visitors Chipping Campden still
retains much of its old-world charm.

Lunch was at the Lygon Arms, one of the nicest and most authentic pubs
in the centre of the town. The Lygon Arms has traditionally hosted the
opening hunt meet and the landlord is especially friendly and welcoming to
riders. He has even gone so far as to put rails up at the back of the pub so
that horses can be tied up safely.

After lunch we rode our horses out through the archway of the hotel
front and into the high street, riding on past the famous Woolstaplers' Hall

Heading up the hill
to Norton Hall after a
long day.

Opposite: The sunlight
catches the soft limestone
buildings of Chipping
Campden.

which dates from 1340. Under its arches merchants from as far away as Florence bargained for the famous Cotswold wool.

When on horseback you get a quite a different perspective of a town than from a car or on foot. Peering through windows and over walls everything looks quite new, though this is, of course, exactly the way our forbears would have seen the town.

A short distance from Chipping Campden we turned off to Dover's Hill. Owned by the National Trust it has magnificent views northwards and westwards – on good days as far as the Brecon Beacons in Wales. The ground was icy and hard and the horses slid and slipped as we picked our way over the frosty ground up to the summit of the hill. There was not a cloud in the sky and the luminescent winter light gave the far-reaching views a fairy-tale quality.

We rode down off Dover's Hill and into the parklands of Burnt Norton,

Above: The fairytale frost that covers Dover's Hill is enhanced by the winter light.

Above right: Approaching Foxcote House in the late afternoon.

Right: Heading home as the sun begins to set.

another historic Cotswold house from the Victorian period, before crossing the railway line and entering the beautiful park of Norton Hall, where we were to be spending our second night. Home to the Pollen family, Norton Hall is an impressive early Victorian house. Riding up the driveway we were greeted by the children who led us excitedly down to the Lake Field where the horses were to be turned out. Twenty-five years ago Marcus Pollen's father began planting rare and exotic trees all over the park. The result today is an amazing arboretum.

Norton Hall is romantic. Everything is faded and slightly falling apart. Children's toys are scattered along the landings and piles of clothes heaped up on the kitchen table. But the atmosphere is fun and relaxed. Dinner that night was a delicious oxtail soup cooked by Marcus and served in the kitchen. Later, having consumed quite a few bottles of wine, we made our way up to our vast bedrooms and collapsed gratefully into bed.

'The horse, with beauty unsurpassed, strength immeasurable and grace unlike any other, still remains humble enough to carry a man upon his back.' – Amber Senti

DAY 2 - Norton Hall to Admington (13 miles)

The bright sunshine streamed in through the enormous sash windows of the bedroom waking us up. Outside was a winter wonderland with the countryside shrouded in a delicate white frost.

　　After breakfast we headed off past the stables down the back drive and the long track towards Mickleton village. We crossed over the busy village street and passing the church headed into a deep-sided valley until Kiftsgate House came into view. Kiftsgate is home to the famous rose, a climbing vigorous white variety planted in 1938, that is supposed to be the largest in Britain, some 90 feet across and 50 feet high.

From the valley we emerged through some stone pillars onto a small lane and then straight across the road to Hidcote. Amazingly two great gardens are within a stone throw of one another. Unfortunately, however it was winter and both were closed for the season. Hidcote, though, is considered to be one of the most important gardens in the country. Designed by Major Lawrence Johnston in the early part of the century, it was the first garden to taken on by the National Trust. A self-taught gardener, Johnston was clearly a genius and his creation is an inspiration for garden designers all over the world. Having transformed all the fields around his house, by 1920 Johnston had twelve full-time gardeners working for him. After years of careful selection Johnston eventually came up with the narrow-leaved lavender, Lavandula angustifolia, or Hidcote as it came to be known.

The Howard Arms, Ilmington: the perfect place to tie up the horses and stop for lunch.

The next part of our journey took us on down some lanes and a coppice wood until eventually we emerged on Stoke Hill, once again overlooking Foxcote House. The bridleway took us down the hill towards the house and at the end of the long driveway we turned left, heading down the small lane towards the Howard Arms at Illmington for lunch. This is an exceptionally nice gourmet pub which caters to riders by allowing them to tie up their horses to some railings at the back. The food is delicious and the atmosphere friendly and warm. There is always a nice fire, which was especially welcome on this freezing February day.

After lunch, we left the village and turned right up Pig Lane. At the top the road forked and we cantered over the fields and back to Admington. Riding back into the beautiful cobbled stable block we were met by Antonia's groom, Elias. Leaving the horses with him, we wandered into the house where there was a delicious pot of China tea and a plate of brown toast with Gentleman's Relish waiting for us on a silver platter! How English, we thought to ourselves, and what a fitting end to our ride through the Heart of England.

THE COTSWOLDS

The Cotswolds is an area of gentle hillsides, sleepy villages and famous market towns. With both buildings and dry stone walls constructed of the same honey-coloured local limestone the area has a uniformity of architecture that makes the Cotswolds a favourite location for visitors from all over the world.

Our first night was spent just outside the town of Stow-on-the-Wold in a lovely farmhouse called Banks Fee. Arriving up the long driveway we passed through an archway into a magnificent stable yard. Three or four hunters looked out over the stable doors at us as we unpacked our bags and went into the house to meet our hosts, Annie and Christopher Cox. Their house is a testament to their passion for horses and their love of the countryside. Paintings of their horses decorate the walls and every photograph has someone jumping a hedge.

Riding past the frosty churchyard in the aptly named village of Snowshill.

DAY 1 - Stow-on-the-Wold to Broadway (13 miles)

It was bitterly cold when we rode out of the stable yard the following
morning with Fred, Annie's huge hunter, polished to a mahogany sheen,
looking eagerly over his stable door. We passed through Condicote, a small
village nestled in a shallow dip and sheltered from the biting winds of the
surrounding hills. A narrow lane wound on to Hinchwick. All was quiet,
nothing but the clip clop of hooves and the screeching of rooks overhead.
Hinchwick Manor is one of the last of the great Cotswold houses to have
avoided a 20th-century makeover and stands discreetly behind fading walls.
The old carriage turning circle provided a convenient lay-by from which to
stop and peer up through a high archway at a lovely and unspoilt example of
17th century vernacular architecture.

Just past the manor we entered a field, which led us into a haven known
locally as Happy Valley. With soft green hills folding gently into one another
and ancient beech woods towering on either side, this lovely valley always
seems sheltered and even on this cold day the sun seemed to settle on us.

Above: The bare trees and ploughed fields
of Gloucestershire in mid-January.
Below: Riding up Happy Valley.

Otto and Picasso rest in the stableyard at Banks Fee.

Childswickham

Manor Farm

Leverton

Wormington Grange

Stanton

Broadway Tower

Snowshill

Stanway

Paper Mill Farm

Buckle Street

Happy Valley

Stumps Cross

Hinchwick

Condicote

Lynes Barn Farm

Bank Fee Farm

Kineton

Guiting Manor

OS Landranger 150 and 151

Crossing Buckle Street, an old Roman road, the landscape around us opened up – the newly seeded fields dissected by crumbling stonewalls – as we made our way down to the picture-postcard village of Snowshill. In the early 20th century it was a honeypot for the Bloomsbury set who spent long weekends at the Manor as guests of the eccentric Charles Paget Wade. Virginia Woolf, Graham Greene and J.B. Priestly would have been among those entertained in the Manor, now a National Trust property situated at

Looking through the mist across the valley towards Broadway Tower.

the heart of the village. Snowshill is a village in which time seems to have stood still.

After a delicious lunch with Fleur Sladen we left Snowshill behind us clinging to the frosty hillside, smoke rising in tendrils from chimney pots and took an old path out of the village; ahead were sweeping views of the Vale of Evesham. Heading out on the lanes towards Childswickham where we were to spend the night we saw the famous Broadway Tower standing like a singular chess piece high on top of the hill.

At Manor Farm, our hostess, Marion Houghton, appeared as if from nowhere as we clip clopped into the driveway with a tray of tea and cake. A little later, after we turned the horses out into a ridge-and-furrow field behind the house listed in the Domesday Book. We walked into the hallway and were under no illusions as to the real passion in the lives of Marion and her husband, Christopher: hanging up are dozens of well-worn hunting jackets above row upon row of shiny black boots. This tradition goes back to Christopher's father who was the Broadway doctor for 50 years and hunted twice a week on the same horse he used to visit his patients. Christopher is dashing and generous – his favourite pastime is to take guests off on a whirlwind tour of the beautiful town of Broadway in his immaculate 1920s open top Bentley.

Right: The hallway at Manor Farm is a shrine to hunting.

Overleaf: The undulating, sunbathed hills of Happy Valley.

DAY 2 - Broadway to Wormington (9 miles)

After breakfast we made our way towards the village of Laverton where we began our climb up the escarpment and on to the Cotswold Way. Looking back at the extraordinary views to the west we could see as far as the Malverns and beyond to Wales. On reaching the top we rode in a straight line along the edge of the escarpment, the winter wind biting at our faces. We were relieved to turn down into the shelter of Stanway Wood. Along the way we past the tiny shepherd's hut where Ben Kingsley filmed the 1985 production of George Eliot's *Silas Marner*.

We turned off by a gamekeeper's cottage towards Paper Mill Farm. An old-fashioned farm, it sits below the bridleway in its own small valley. The confusion of farm implements, manure heaps, and a hillside covered with Devon Red cattle suggested a farming tenancy in full swing.

Riding into the heart of Lidcombe Woods the horses were spooked by the eerie echo of a mechanical water pump which has been echoing through the woods for over 180 years. In spring the smell of wild garlic is overwhelming but on this cold February day the banks were dormant. The path through the wood was steep and stony so the horses were relieved to emerge into the fields of Shenberrow before heading down to the beautifully preserved village of Stanton.

Above: Our route took us north along the Cotswold Way.

Below: From the top of an escarpment we overlooked the Vale of Evesham and the Malvern Hills beyond.

Opposite, left: At times we passed through ancient beech woods.

Opposite, right: The drive at Wormington Grange passes through an avenue of young trees.

The Mount Pub, where we stopped for lunch is perched high up on the hill with panoramic views out to the Malvern Hills. The afternoon ride was only a short distance away so we relaxed over a few glasses of wine and local cider, a rather bewitching combination, before we remounted and hazily picked our way through the honey-coloured cottages of Stanton to the lodge and drive of Wormington Grange. Approached down a long, straight, tree-lined driveway, polo ponies were turned out for winter grazed in the fields on

either side. The house, when it came into view looked like something out of a
Brontë novel – any moment we expected Mr Darcy to come cantering up on a
prancing black horse. Built on the site of an ancient abbey the house was
extended and renovated extensively in the early 20th century. With large
sash windows reaching to the ground it is imposing and grand.

We could have been part of a
Jane Austen novel as we arrived
at Wormington Grange.

DAY 3 - Worminton to Stow (14 miles)

Still cold but brighter and less windy, the morning's ride took us down the
lane which curves quietly under the hill from Stanton to Stanway.
Traditional iron railings stretch for two miles or so between the two villages
and in summer cattle laze under great oak and ash trees. The first sign that
we were close to Stanway House, an outstanding example of a beautiful
Jacobean manor, was a glimpse of the thatched roof of its cricket pavilion.
Raised up on staddle stones and commissioned by the novelist Sir James
Barry it is remains a centre of frenetic mowing and parish sportsmanship.

   Once again the benefits of being up in the saddle allowed us a good
glimpse of the house from the back drive. The jewel-like gatehouse, the
church, the 14th century tithe barn, the 18th century water gardens all set
in ancient parkland make Stanway unique and totally romantic. Owned by
the Wemyss family for five hundred years, the interior of the house is as
extraordinary as the exterior. Priceless pieces of furniture, much of which

Passing Guiting Manor, the perfect Cotswold house.

Crunching through a winter carpet of beech leaves.

has been there since the house was built, decorate the rooms, the bookshelves are filled with first editions and yet the carpets are threadbare and the paint is peeling. The 21st Century has not infringed upon the beauty of Stanway. Lord Wemyss rents out the estate cottages and farms to locals enabling them to remain in what has become one of the most exclusive and expensive areas of England.

The old roadway, known as Campden Lane, took us towards the small town of Winchcombe and then on down a meandering river valley through the Guiting estate. A haven for wildlife now run as a conservation trust, it is a shining example of modern land management and conservation – and has received numerous awards for its success. We rode along a stony track with a stream beside us for a mile or so until the landscape opened up and we emerged into undulating countryside and rolling hills. In front of us was Guiting Manor, a Georgian house with perfect proportions.

We stopped for lunch at the pub in the village of Kineton and then made our way back along the White Way, an ancient salt road that runs from Droitwich to Cirencester. The rush of the hunt could be discerned from many hoof prints either side of impressive jumps carved into the walls – the 'thrusters' way through this fast piece of country.

It was only a little later that we hit the old roman road we had ridden on two days earlier, returning us to Condicote and Banks Fee where tea and toast were waiting.

GLOSSARY

The Great Estates

Places to Stay

Carol Goddard
Landage House, Rendcomb,
Cirencester GL7 7HB
01285 831250
carol.landage@tiscali.co.uk

Melissa Kennedy
The Old Rectory, Miserden,
Stroud GL6 7JA
01285 821165
billy.kennedy@yahoo.co.uk

Sheila Platt
Upcote Farm, Withington,
Cheltenham GL54 4BL
01242 890250

Places to Eat

The Bell, Sapperton
01285 760298
www.foodatthebell.co.uk

The Green Dragon Inn, Cockleford
01242 870271
www.green-dragon-inn.co.uk

The Seven Tuns, Chedworth
01285 720 242

Places to Visit

The Roman Villa, Chedworth
01242 890256
www.nationaltrust.org.ukchedworth-
roman-villa

Miserden Park Gardens, Miserden
01285 821303
www.misardenpark.co.uk

Painswick Rococo Garden, Painswick
01452 813204
www.rococogarden.org.uk

Guided Rides

Greenhill Equitation, Daglingworth
01285 644982
www.greenhillequitation.com

Farriers

David Dawson
07968 734679

David Hall
07831 261438

Vet

Woodland Vets, Cheltenham
01242 255133

Top: The Bell, Sapperton
Above: Melissa Kennedy
Right: Sheila and John Platt

North-west Norfolk

Places to Stay

Lower Farm, Back Street, Harpley,
King's Lynn PE31 6TU
01485 520240
www.lowerfarmholidaycottages.co.uk

Barry and Valerie Southerland
Whitehall Farm, Burnham Thorpe,
Burnham Market PE31 8HN
01328 738416
www.whitehallfarm-accommodation.com

Places to Eat

Bircham Windmill and Tea Rooms,
Bircham
01485 578393
www.birchamwindmill.co.uk

Places to Eat in the Evening

The Rose and Crown, Harpley
01485 520577

The Lord Nelson, Burnham Thorpe
01328 738241
www.nelsonslocal.co.uk

Places to Visit

Creake Abbey
07801 418907
www.creakeabbey.co.uk

Houghton Hall
01485 528 569
www.houghtonhall.com

Holkham Beach and Nature Reserve
01328 711183
www.holkham.co.uk

Horse Hire and Guided Rides

Blackborough End Equestrian Centre,
Narford, Kings Lynn
01553 841212
www.beec.co.uk

Farriers

Anvil Farm Farriers, Syderstone,
Kings Lynn 01485 578241

Hill Beck Barn Farriers, East Winch,
Kings Lynn 01533 840425

Vet

Norfolk Equine Veterinary Services,
Kings Lynn 01485 600260
www.norfolkequinevet.co.uk

Top: The deer park, Houghton Hall
Below: Barry and Valerie Southerland

Zara, the groom

Exmoor

Places to Stay

Stockleigh Lodge, Minehead TA24 7PZ
01643 831500
www.stockleighexford.co.uk

Jennifer and Alan Thomas
Higher Rodhuish Farm, Rodhuish,
Minehead TA24 6QL
01984 640253
Jennifer@thomas2008B.Entadsl.com

Emmett's Grange House,
Simonsbath, Minehead TA24 7LD
0845 6805431
www.emmettsgrange.co.uk

Places to Eat

The Rest and Be Thankful Inn,
Wheddon Cross
01643 841222
www.restandbethankful.co.uk

The Royal Oak, Withypool
01643 831506
www.royaloakwithypool.co.uk

Places to Visit

St Bartholomew's Church, Rodhuish

Lorna Doone Country,
Exmoor National Park
Exmoor National Park Authority
01398 323665
www.exmoor-nationalpark.gov.uk

Farrier

Kent and Son, Minehead
01643 831264

Vets

Charter Veterinary Hospital Group,
Barnstaple, Braunton and Ilfracombe
01271 371115
www.chartervets.com

Wolfgar Veterinary Group,
Cheriton Bishop
01647 24232
www.wolfgarvets.co.uk

Top: The Thomas family
Left: Jake at the Royal Oak
St. Bartholomew's Church, Rodhuish

Hardy's Dorset

Places to Stay

Jenny Needham
Wyndham House, Buckland Newton,
Dorchester DT2 7BL
01300 345534
jenny.needham@kmc.ac.uk

Louly Thorneycroft
Fivepenny House, Shillingstone Lane,
Okeford Fitzpaine, Blandford DT11 0RD
01258 860614

Sarah Clarke
Fishmore Hill Farm,
Milton Abbas DT11 0DL
01258 881122
www.fishmorehillfarm.com

Places to Eat

The Hambro Arms, Milton Abbas
01258 880233
www.hambroarms.com

The Needham family

The Brace of Pheasants, Plush
01300 348357
www.braceofpheasants.co.uk

Place to Eat in the Evening

Lulworth Cove Inn and Restaurant,
Lulworth Cove
01929 400333
www.lulworth-coveinn.co.uk

Places to Visit

Hardy's Cottage, Brockhampton
01208 869247
www.nationaltrust.org.uk

Max Gate, Dorchester
01305 262538
www.nationaltrust.org.uk

Milton Abbas: a cob and thatch village

Beaches at Lulworth Cove, Durdle Door
and Chesil Beach
www.nationaltrust.co.uk

Horse Hire and Guided Rides

Steph Buchanan, RAC Saddle Club,
Bovington
01929 403580
www.racsaddleclub.co.uk

Farriers

Pete Coutanche, Weymouth
07980 623486

Bailey Mobile Shoeing, Blandford Forum
01258 452649

Vet

Whistlejacket Equine Veterinary Surgery,
Milton Abbas
01258 881777
www.whistlejacketvet.co.uk

Louly Thorneycroft

The Vale of Belvoir

Places to Stay

Mrs Camilla Murdoch
Sewstern Grange, Sewstern,
Grantham NG33 5RW
01572 787463
sewsterngrange@tiscali.co.uk

Manners Arms, Croxton Road, Knipton
NG32 1RH
01476 879222
www.mannersarms.com

Places to Eat

The Nags Head, Saltby
01476 860491

The Wheel Inn, Branston
01476 870376
www.thewheelinnbranston.co.uk

The Rutland Arms (or 'Dirty Duck'),
Woolsthorpe
01476 870360

Places to Eat in the Evening

The Tollemache Arms, Buckminster
01476 860477
www.tollemache-arms.co.uk

The Berkeley Arms, Wymondham
01572 787587
www.theberkeleyarms.co.uk

Places to Visit

Belvoir Castle
01476 871002
www.belvoircastle.com

Belton House, Grantham
01476 566116
www.nationaltrust.org.uk

Rutland Water
01780 686800
www.rutlandwater.org.uk

Riding Centres

Somerby Equestrian Centre,
Melton Mowbray
01664 454838
www.somerbyequestriancentre.co.uk

Stretton Riding and Training Centre,
Oakham
01780 410323

Farrier

Jonathan Allington, Melton Mowbray
07970 417037

Vet

Tower Equine, Grimsthorpe
01778 591082
www.towerequine.co.uk

Top: Belvoir Castle
Left: The Duchess of Rutland

The Welsh Borders

Places to Stay

Judy and Chris Menges
Fron Farm, Dutlas, Knighton LD7 1RH
01547 510276
Judy@fronfilm.com

John Underwood and John Rath
Cwmllechwedd Fawr, Llanbister LD1 6UH
01597 840267
www.cwmllechweddfawr.co.uk

Brandy House Farm, Felindre,
Knighton LD7 1YL
01547 510282
www.brandyhousefarm.co.uk

Places to Eat

The Waterdine Inn, Llanfair Waterdine,
Knighton
01547 528214

Places to Visit

Powis Castle and Garden, Welshpool
01938 551944
www.nationaltrust.org.uk

Ludlow Castle
01584 874465
www.ludlowcastle.com

Farriers

Tom Booth, Knighton
01547 520605

Rob Duggan, Knighton
01547 550301

Vet

Ashburn Veterinary Centre, Knighton
01547 529600
www.ashburnveterinarycentre.co.uk

Top: Fron Farm
Left: The Two Johns
Below: Cwmllechwedd Fawr

Cranborne Chase

Places to Stay

Tina Yarrow
Boveridge Farm, Cranborne BH21 5RU
01725 517447

Josie Green
Cromwell Manor, Sutton Mandeville,
Salisbury SP3 5ND
01722 714645
josegreen2011@gmail.com

Ailsa Macleod
Tenantry Farm, Rockbourn,
Fordingbridge SP6 3PB
01725 518297

Places to Eat

The Queens Head, Broadchalke
01722 780344
www.thequeensheadbroadchalke.co.uk

The Horseshoe Inn, Ebbesbourne Wake
01962 732859

Places to Eat in the Evening

The Compasses, Lower Chicksgrove
01722 714318
www.thecompassesinn.com

The King John, Tollard Royale
01725 516207
www.kingjohninn.co.uk

Places to Visit

Old Wardour Castle, Nr Tisbury
(bridleway access)
01747 870487
www.english-heritage.org.uk

Wilton House, Stourhead
01722 746714
www.wiltonhouse.com

Farrier

Steve Griffin, Chicksgrove
07799 866047

Vet

Endell Veterinary Group, Salisbury
01722 333291

*Top: Boveridge Farm
Below, left to right: Tina Yarrow,
The Greens, Ailsa Macleod*

The Yorkshire Moors

Places to Stay

Karen Ridley
Manor Farm, Newton-upon-Rawcliffe,
Pickering YO18 8QA
01284 763568
www.manorfarmcottagesnewton.com

Catriona Cook
Burgate Farm, Harwood Dale,
Scarborough YO13 0DS
01723 870333

Barbara Tyerman
Partridge Nest Farm, Eskdaleside,
Whitby YO22 5ES
01947 810450
www.partridgenestfarm.com

Penny Richardson
High Farm, Newholm, Whitby YO21 3QY
01947 600371

Places to Eat

Saltersgate Inn
01751 460237

Moorcock Inn, Langdale End
01723 882268

Birch Hall Inn, Beck Hole
01947 896245
www.beckhole.info/bhi.htm

The Inn on the Moor,
Goathland
01947 896296
www.innonthemoor.co.uk

Places to Visit

Castle Howard, York
01653 648333
www.castlehoward.co.uk

Whitby Abbey
01947 603568
www.english-heritage.org.uk

Horse Hire and Guided Rides

Friars Hill Stables
Friars Hill, York YO62 6SL
01751 432758

Farriers

Duncan Smith, Scarborough
01723 375947

Danny Bentley
07855 326846

Vets

Cundall and Duffy, Scarborough
01723 375947
www.cundallduffyvets.co.uk

The Beck Veterinary Practice, Whitby
01947 820333
www.whitbyvet.co.uk

Catriona Cook

The Surrey Sussex Commons

Places to Stay

Jill Collins
Eden Cottage, Tilford Road,
Rushmore GU10 2EB
01252 792195

Nicky and John Braithwaite
Lower House Farm, Ropes Lane,
Fernhurst, Haslemere GU27 3JD
01428 656923

Heath Hall Farm, Bowlhead Green,
Thursley, Godalming GU8 6NW
01428 682808
www.heathhallfarm.co.uk

Places to Eat

The Dog and Pheasant, Brook
01428 682763
www.dogandpheasant.com

The Duke of Cambridge, Tilford
01252 792 236
www.dukeofcambridgetilford.co.uk

The Barley Mow, Tilford Green, Farnham
01252 792205
ww.thebarleymowtilford.com

Farriers

M. Taylor, Hindhead
07831 836932

Ralph Tucker, Petworth
01428 707184

Vet

Southern Hill Equine Vets, Guildford
01483 811007
www.southernhillsequine.com

Horse Hire and Guided Rides

Joyce Whatley
Rural Rides, Blackdown Riding Club,
Fernhurst
01428 654106
www.ruralridesuk.co.uk

Top: Lower House Farm
Below, left: Nicky and John Braithwaite
Below: The Medici bed at Lower House
Farm

The Shropshire Hills

Places to Stay

Nicky Caden
Dudgeley Farm, Lower Wood,
All Stretton SY6 6LE
07771 762939 or 07773 553345
nicky@dudgeleyfarm.co.uk

Timothy Rawdon-Mogg
Stone Cottage, The Bog,
Minsterley SY5 ONJ
01743 792073 or 0751 8433774
timrm@pennerley.net

The Stiperstones Inn,
Stiperstones SY5 0LZ
Tel:01743 791327
www.stiperstonesinn.co.uk

Guided Rides

Helen Foster
01694 771283
Helen_jonty_broome@hotmail.com

Farriers

Tom Williamson, Church Stretton
01694 722767

Oliver Roberts, Dorrington
07792 707220

Vets

Stretton Hills Equine Vet Practice,
All Stretton
07855 365941
www.strettonhillsveterinarypractice.co.uk

Top: Dudgeley Farm
Left: Helen Foster
Below: Timothy Rawton-Mogg, the
'Galloping Vicar'

The Heart of England

Unfortunately we cannot give the contact details of the private homes we stayed in along the way. If you wish to do this ride with us, contact us at:
Stately Rides
07590 456714
www.statelyrides.co.uk
charlottesp@btconnect.com

Alternatively, use the following information to help you organize your own ride:

Places to Stay

Gaynor Brundle
Mickleton Hills Farm, Furze Lane,
Chipping Campden GL55 6LJ
01386 841939

Christine Spencer
Vicarage Farm, Lower Quinton,
Stratford-upon-Avon CV37 8RY
01789 721108

Places to Eat

The Lygon Arms, Chipping Campden
01386 840318
www.lygonarms.co.uk

Top: Antonia Davies, Admington Hall
Below: The Howard Arms

The Howard Arms, Ilmington
01608 682226
www.howardarms.com

Places to Visit

Hidcote Manor Gardens,
Chipping Camden
01386 438333
www.nationaltrust.org.uk/hidcote/

Kiftsgate Court Gardens,
Chipping Camden
01386 438777
www.kiftsgate.co.uk

Royal Shakespeare Company,
Stratford-upon-Avon
Ticketline: 0844 800 1110
www.rsc.org.uk

Horse Hire

Jill Carenza, Cotswold Riding,
Welshpool Riding Centre, Stanton
01386 584250
www.cotswoldsriding.co.uk

Coreen Miller
07946 490843

Farriers

Sean Whelan, Rugby
07766 460566

Tom Heath
07881 868007

Vets

Corner House Equine, Henley-in-Arden
01564 743033
www.cornerhousevets.com

Avondale Veterinary, Banbury
01295 670501

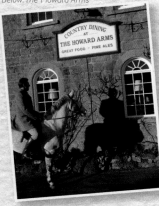

The Cotswolds

Unfortunately we cannot give the contact details of the private homes we stayed in along the way. If you wish to do this ride with us, contact us at:
Stately Rides
07590 456714
www.statelyrides.co.uk
charlottesp@btconnect.com

Alternatively, use the following information to help you organize your own ride:

Places to Stay

Ann Flavell-Wood (alongside Woodlands Riding Stables)
Wood-Stanway, Cheltenham GL54 5PG
01386 584752
annflavellwood@yahoo.co.uk

Jill Carenza (also horses for hire and guided rides)
The Vine, Stanton, Broadway WR12 7NE
01386 584250
cotswoldsriding@yahoo.co.uk

Westward, Sudeley,
Winchcombe GL54 5JB
01242 604372
www.westward-sudeley.co.uk

Places to Eat

The Snowshill Arms, Snowshill
01386 852653
www.donnington-brewery.com/
pub_snowshill.php

The Mount Inn, Stanton
01386 584316
www.themountinn.co.uk

The Halfway House, Kineton
01451 850344
www.thehalfwayhousekineton.co.uk

Places to Eat in the Evening

Wesley House, Winchcombe
01242 602366
www.wesleyhouse.co.uk

Buckland Manor Hotel, Buckland
01386 852626
www.bucklandmanor.co.uk

Places to Visit

Stanway House and Fountain, Stanway
01386 584469
www.stanwayfountain.co.uk

Snowshill Manor, Snowshill
01386 842814
www.nationaltrust.org.uk/snowshill-manor

Horse Hire and Guided Rides

Jill Carenza, Cotswold Riding,
Welshpool Riding Centre, Stanton
01386 584250
www.cotswoldsriding.co.uk

Woodlands Riding Stables, Winchcombe
01386 584404
www.woodstanway.co.uk

Farriers

Julian Day
07768 961051

Ben Howson
07747 155255

Vet

Peasebrook Equine Clinic, Broadway
01386 853884
www.peasebrookequineclinic.com

Top, left: Annie Dowty, Wormington Grange
Top, right: Fleur Sladen, Snowshill
Below, left: Annie Cox, Banks Fee
Below, right: Marion Houghton, Manor Farm

FURTHER INFORMATION

For more information on routes, maps and rides contact England on Horseback at
www.englandonhorseback.co.uk.

For guided rides contact us at www.statelyrides.co.uk.

ACKNOWLEDGEMENTS

We could not have made these incredible journeys around England without the extraordinary
help of so many people who had us to stay along the way.

We would particularly like to thank Catriona Cook, an inspiration for all long-distance riders,
Helen Foster who so kindly took us on a two-day ride across the most beautiful parts of
Shropshire, Tracey and Richard Martin who led us for three days across some of the most
untouched parts of Surrey, Jenny Needham who was so helpful in coming up with suggestions for
rides, Bobbie Matulja for opening up the world of long-distance riding to us, Lianne Souter for
her care and commitment to our horses, Jake Calvert, Hunter Boots Ltd for their footwear,
Barbour for the jackets we wore on our journeys, Catharine Snow at Clearview Books for making
our dream become a reality and Susannah English for creating such beautiful maps of our rides.

None of this would have been possible without the constant help, understanding and love of our
families. A special thanks to Jonty Colchester for all his support, enthusiasm and editorial input,
Esme, Mac, Ned and Bertie Sainsbury-Plaice for being so patient when their mother took off
around the countryside and to both our mothers who introduced us to riding – thank you.

But finally, a special thanks to our hero, A.F. Tschiffely, who wrote the book *Bridle Paths* in 1936
which inspired and encouraged us to go off on our jaunts around England, and, last but not least,
Charlie, Picasso, Murphy, Marble, Star and Otto, our four-legged friends who transported us
so patiently across the countryside.